Henri Nouwen

A SPIRITUALITY OF IMPERFECTION

Wil Hernandez

PAULIST PRESS
New York/Mahwah, N.J.

Unless otherwise noted, the scripture quotations outlined herein are from the New Revised Standard Version Bible, copyright © 1989 by the Division of Christian Education of the National Council of Churches of Christ in the U.S.A. Used by permission.

Excerpt on page 7 taken from T. S. Eliot, "East Coker," in *The Complete Poems and Plays: 1909–1950* (New York: Harcourt Brace & Co., 1952).

Excerpt on page 73 taken from Wallace Stevens, "Poems of Our Climate," in *The Collected Poems of Wallace Stevens* (New York: Alfred A. Knopf, 1954).

Cover design by Joel Dasalla
Book design by Lynn Else

Copyright © 2006 by The Leadership Institute

Library of Congress Cataloging-in-Publication Data

Hernandez, Wil.
    Henri Nouwen : a spirituality of imperfection / Wil Hernandez.
    p. cm.
    ISBN 0-8091-4434-4 (alk. paper)
    1. Nouwen, Henri J. M. 2. Spiritual life—Catholic Church. 3. Spiritual formation. 4. Nouwen, Henri J. M. 5. Perfection—Religious aspects—Catholic Church. I. Title.
    BX2350.3.H47 2006
    248.4'82—dc22

                                                    2006023984

Published by Paulist Press
997 Macarthur Boulevard
Mahwah, New Jersey 07430

www.paulistpress.com

Printed and bound in the
United States of America

To Dave W.,
*my soul brother who, like Henri Nouwen,
authentically lives out
a spirituality of imperfection*

Contents

Foreword

Michael J. Christensen

There are many ways to describe Christian spirituality, the journey of faith, and the movements of the Spirit. Ancient Judaism understood the Spirit as the blowing of the *wind* of God. Similarly, in the Christian tradition, the wind of the Spirit is the *breath* of God. Both the Hebrew word *ruach* and the Greek word *pneuma* mean "wind, or breath." Living a spiritual life, then, is *breathing with the life and breath of God*, who is within us and among us.

The Spirit blows where it wants to blow and leads us in wholly unexpected ways. While the Spirit is free to breathe and blow and work in our life in unique and mysterious ways, there are many tried and tested ways in Christian tradition of responding to the Wind that help us live a spiritual life. These practices Henri Nouwen calls spiritual disciplines, and taken together form the movements in the journey of faith in which we are invited to participate according to our capacity and charism.

Drawing on Elizabeth O'Connor's book *Journey Inward, Journey Outward,* Nouwen understood the spiritual life as a journey inward to the heart and a journey outward in community and mission. Nouwen says,

> The journey inward is the journey to find the Christ dwelling within us. The journey outward is the journey to find the

Michael J. Christensen, PhD, teaches spirituality and religious studies at Drew University, where he also directs the doctor of ministry program. He is coauthor of Spiritual Direction: Wisdom for the Long Walk of Faith *by Henri Nouwen (HarperCollins, 2006).*

Christ dwelling among us and in the world. The journey inward in communion requires the disciplines of solitude, silence, prayer, meditation, contemplation, and attentiveness to the movements of our heart. The journey outward in community and mission requires the disciplines of care, compassion, witness, outreach, healing, accountability, and attentiveness to the movement of other people's hearts. These two journeys belong together to strengthen each other, and should never be separated.[1]

In this welcome volume, *Henri Nouwen: A Spirituality of Imperfection*, Wil Hernandez adds an important element to Nouwen's journey motif: The spiritual journey is not only a journey inward (via psychology) and a journey outward (in ministry); it also is a journey upward to God (doing theology) in combining faith and practice. Carefully articulating how Christian theology is infused with spirituality, Hernandez makes explicit Nouwen's implicit understanding of theological reflection as a necessary discipline of spiritual practice. "Following Thomas Merton," Hernandez writes in this volume, "Henri Nouwen adopted the style of personal narration to reflect critically on himself [and God] and to mesh his thought and action." In theological reflection, "one's personal experience is examined from a decidedly Christian grid for the express purpose of transformation..." In so doing, theological reflection for Nouwen is a tool to "consciously bridge the gap between his *professed* and *expressed* theology— between what he believed and how he actually functioned in life. In fact, Nouwen's decision to move to L'Arche was said to be driven by a desire to close the gap between what he wrote and what he lived." Thus, *theologia* is a conscious movement upward to God in active prayer and critical reflection for the purpose of spiritual transformation in faith and practice.

Systematic reflection on Nouwen's understanding of the threefold journey of faith reveals that there are many transformative movements within each journey (inward, outward, and upward). The dynamics of the journey, identified as the many movements along the way, are movements from *this* quality to *that*, from something enslaving and destructive to something liberating and life-giving. He developed this familiar pattern at

Notre Dame, and continued using it at Yale and Harvard as well as in books throughout his teaching and writing career. For example, in his first book, *Pray to Live* (now *Thomas Merton: Contemplative Critic*), the movement is from sarcasm to contemplation, and from opaqueness to transparency.

In subsequent books, Nouwen identified other movements of the spiritual life. In *Reaching Out*, he identified three, each with a corresponding discipline: The first movement is from loneliness to solitude, requiring the discipline of silence; the second is from hostility to hospitality, inviting the discipline of ministry; the third movement is from illusion to the prayer of the heart, requiring both contemplative prayer and community discernment.

In *Making All Things New*, there is the movement from alienation to community. In *Compassion*, it's from competition to compassion. In *Creative Ministry*, from a violent to a redemptive way of learning, and from professionalism to creative ministry. In *Here and Now*, the many movements include from fatalism to faith, from worrying to prayer, and from mind to heart. In *The Name of Jesus*, from relevance to prayer, from popularity to ministry, and from leading to being led. In *The Inner Voice of Love*, the movement is from anguish to freedom. *In Lifesigns*, the movement is from the house of fear to the house of love. In *The Return of the Prodigal Son*, the three movements are from dissipation to homecoming, from bitterness to gratitude, and from forgiven to forgiver. And in *Our Greatest Gift*, the final movement in the human journey is from aging to dying.

These predictable movements of the Spirit vary with the individual and community of faith, and are never static, absolute, or perfectly completed, as if we could graduate from one movement to another before continuing our journey. Rather, we are always in the process of discerning which way the wind is blowing, seeking to breathe with Spirit's rhythm, and moving in the right direction on the long journey of faith. This paradigm, of course, is rooted in the Jewish experience of the exodus from bondage to freedom; and in the Christian experience of salvation from death to life in progressive stages of *illumination, purgation,* and *unification* with God.

In *Henri Nouwen: A Spirituality of Imperfection*, Wil Hernandez again makes a bold contribution to how best to understand the journey of faith and the many movements along the way. Examining Nouwen's own movements, Hernandez characterizes the spiritual journey as "a spirituality of imperfection." By this he means a *relational* spirituality of intimacy with God and a faithful wrestling with God that gradually ripens into a mature communion or "completeness" with the Divine; this, rather than a *conforming* spirituality of moral perfectionism and victory over sin that progressively takes on the characterological likeness to God's perfect nature. Inward transformation does lead to outward conformity to God's image and likeness, but moral striving for such perfection is the antithesis to Nouwen's spirituality of imperfection.

For Nouwen, spiritual "perfection" is a dynamic quality of relational "completeness" found in resting one's head in the bosom of the Father, abiding in the intimate love between the Father and the Son, or hearing the inner voice of God call you "the beloved." Such sweet communion does not automatically result in a perfection of character, victory over sin, or consistently right actions. But this is not what Christ commands in the Gospel of Matthew when he says: "Be ye perfect as your father in heaven is perfect" (Matt 5:48). Luke may have understood Christ better when he renders the phrase: "Be merciful, just as your Father is merciful" (Luke 6:36).

Hernandez comes to this understanding of perfection as completeness and compassion through life experience and by broadening his devout Catholic upbringing and Evangelical experience. His is a familiar story. After years of personal frustration at repeated attempts to "be perfect" and "live a victorious Christian life," he embraced a new spirituality of radical trust in God's transforming love within a wider ecumenism of spiritual practice and a more "generous orthodoxy" of beliefs and practices in relation to sin, salvation, and sanctification. As Hernandez says here: "I found, much to my relief, that deep spirituality can coexist with the sobering realities of imperfection—that the route to perfection is, in fact, through acknowledging one's imperfection."

Thus, the Nouwen that Hernandez sees and writes about through the lens of his own experience and convictions is a morally imperfect but spiritually mature Nouwen as exemplary spiritual director, writer, and priest. Hernandez makes no claim to have captured the "full-orbed picture" of Nouwen's spirituality, but simply offers a "certain portrayal of Henri Nouwen that emerges out of a sustained and thoughtful reading of him"—a spiritual portrait of a "saint" with feet of clay and a heart of gold whose completeness in Christ is through transparent imperfection of all-too-human self.

"Going home is a lifelong journey," writes Nouwen about the spiritual life. "There are always parts of ourselves that wander off in dissipation or get stuck in resentment. Before we know it we are lost..."[2] Brokenness and woundedness are part of what it means to be human. Weakness and vulnerability are part of the strength of our spirituality. The journey of faith is far from smooth or free from errors. The various movements of the spiritual life are never in a straight line or without dissonance and distractions. Spiritual disciplines supported by a faith community help us return to the path and find our true home in God—which is the true spirit of Christian perfection.[3] "As we walk home," Nouwen reminds us, "we often realize how long the way is. But let us not be discouraged. Jesus walks with us and speaks to us on the road. When we listen carefully we discover that we are already home while on the way."[4] *Henri Nouwen: A Spirituality of Imperfection* is a powerful guide for the Christian journey of faith and the various movements of Spirit along the way.

Preface

It all started as a mere curiosity, and a rather mild one at that. One day in class my counseling professor raved about Henri Nouwen's book *The Return of the Prodigal Son*. That was in 1994, back when I was still in the Philippines. Years later, while working on my master's in theology here in the United States, I learned that Nouwen had died two years after my initial "chance encounter" with his work. That was enough to bring him back to my attention.

When I began my PhD program in 1999, I was invited to be a teaching assistant for one of the largest classes at Fuller Seminary. To my surprise, *The Return of the Prodigal Son* was required reading. This unexpected reacquaintance with Nouwen's work turned my once mild curiosity into a growing fascination with his life and work. I did not have to meet Henri Nouwen personally for my interest in him to develop. His books—which I devoured one after another—had a transparent quality that made it easy for me to become familiar with his person.

By the time I entered the second year of my PhD program, I was convinced beyond doubt that my doctoral work would focus on Nouwen. To begin with, my interest in him and his work actually grew out of my own personal journey. In retrospect, the well-used conceptual threads running through most, if not all, of Henri Nouwen's writings—*spirituality, psychology, ministry*, and *theology*—were the same threads that once wove and continue to weave themselves through my own spiritual journey.

At the age of nineteen, I began serving God full-time in *ministry*. The international, interdenominational parachurch organization I joined became for me the "sun" around which my life orbited for eighteen long years. Those were highly productive years for me, but I came to realize that something was missing in my life. I was so outwardly focused that I did not even know who I was anymore. It was at this juncture in my life that I turned inward in order to discover more about myself via the route of counseling and *psychology*. Little did I know that while I was busy ministering to others, my own soul was fast asleep. Busyness provided me a safe shield so that I did not have to face up to who I really was and how I was trying to live my life. I experienced a rude awakening, to say the least. So immersed was I in my new introspective journey that I even thought of becoming a Christian counselor or therapist. But my desperate need for a firmer grounding in God and his word (versus my existential self) led me instead toward the path of *theology*.

It was while studying theology that I became exposed to a lived experience of *spirituality* and spiritual formation. In particular, my immersion into the writings of Henri Nouwen enabled me to realize that true spirituality is dynamically integrated with psychology, ministry, and theology. Indeed, our spiritual journey inevitably consists of an inward, an outward, and an upward reality: a movement toward one's self, toward others, and most importantly, toward God.

I also discovered in Nouwen's writings a particular brand of spirituality that proved to be freeing for me personally. Growing up as a devout Catholic, I spent the first sixteen years of my life striving to reach moral perfection only to fail miserably time and again. Even after having had a taste of the reality of God's grace as a Protestant, I realized how hard it was for old habits to die. For the most part, I still nourished the erroneous thinking that the Christian life was about *being* perfect as opposed to moving toward becoming perfect—however slowly that process might be.

As a growing Christian, I held on to the belief that sustained victory over sin was the norm, and anything less was a substandard lifestyle. The reality of struggle became muted in my own experience since I was led to believe that struggle was not supposed to have a place in a victorious Christian existence. But through the reinforcement of Henri Nouwen's life example I found, much to my relief, that deep spirituality can coexist with the sobering realities of imperfection—that the route to perfection is, in fact, through imperfection.

Thus, as I write about Henri Nouwen, I do so through the lens of my own personal journey. As I seek to understand and interpret Nouwen's perspective, I realize that my interpretation cannot help but be influenced by my own background. Since my work represents but one side of Nouwen—Nouwen as I see him—I can make no claim to being able to sketch a full-orbed picture of his spirituality. Nor do I have the last word concerning it; I believe no one can do that. Just the same, I venture to offer a certain portrayal of Henri Nouwen that emerges out of a sustained and thoughtful reading of him.

Having said all this about my interpretive perspective, I need also to add that I write as a Protestant evangelical with decidedly ecumenical leanings and deep Catholic roots (something which I have recently come to appreciate anew). While remaining loyal to my denomination of preference, I have also reached a point in my journey where issues of denominational differences have become less and less important to me. My appreciation for the wide spectrum of the Body of Christ has increased dramatically as a result of the ecumenically broad exposure that Fuller Seminary has provided for me over the years. I stand convinced that we can, indeed, pursue genuine unity amidst existing diversity within God's church. More than anything, I have personally learned—and I am still learning—to embrace a more "generous orthodoxy" (to borrow the title of Brian McLaren's book) in terms of my beliefs and convictions. To a large extent, this type of spiritual generosity was precisely what Henri Nouwen embodied, being the true ecumenist that he was.

I must also mention that I write this piece of work as an Asian who makes no pretense about being thoroughly conversant with American culture. At the same time, I have lived here now for more than a decade, so I can claim a certain measure of familiarity with the culture that I've chosen to embrace and identify with at this stage in my life. At the risk of sounding presumptuous, I automatically include myself, a Filipino, as part of the American culture when I reference "our" culture in my writing.

In terms of style, I prefer, as much as possible, to dialogue with Henri Nouwen through his writings as if he were alive. Yet I also recognize the challenge of writing in the present tense consistently, especially when certain contexts clearly demand otherwise. It can have a bit of a jarring effect to the reader. Bear with me then as I switch back and forth between the use of the present and the past tense with reference to both Nouwen's life and works.

Henri Nouwen tends to repeat or rehash many of his key ideas in a number of his works. Where appropriate, I have utilized content endnotes and cross-references to point the reader to certain nuances and various other contextual usages of his familiar terms. In employing key terms such as *spirituality, psychology, ministry,* and *theology,* among others, I deal with each term in a more comprehensive manner as it becomes the focal subject of discussion.

When it comes to Henri Nouwen's major writings, I have resorted to parenthetical citation within the text (after initially providing a full citation of a particular work in the endnotes section). The parenthetical citation consists of coded initial(s) of Nouwen's book title followed by page reference(s). For example, (*RO*:12) refers to *Reaching Out: The Three Movements of the Spiritual Life,* page 12. This way we avoid repetitive citations in the endnotes.

Finally, I simply want to say that, overall, this book is about a spiritual journey. It was one that Henri Nouwen himself has taken and with which I intimately identify. In reality, it is a spiritual journey that we all can freely choose to embark upon. This work therefore serves as an open invitation for us to survey its terrain and familiarize ourselves with its contours and textures, with Henri Nouwen as our reliable guide.

Acknowledgments

The production of this book has been a long, arduous journey, but one I traveled with the spiritual accompaniment of special people along the way. It has been a privilege to have the following sacred companions for the past three years while I researched and wrote the book.

First, I want to acknowledge my mentor at Fuller Seminary, Dr. Richard Peace, who patiently guided me through what seemed like an eternal process of giving birth to this final work. I also appreciate Dr. David Augsburger, whose rich insights and generous encouragement spurred me forward in my research.

Thanks also to my ethics professor, Dr. Glen Stassen, who helped readjust my reading of Nouwen so that it reflected more accurately the ethical dimension of Henri Nouwen's spirituality. It was also an honor for me to have Dr. Douglas Burton-Christie of Loyola Marymount University thoughtfully critique the earlier drafts of this work. He, along with my mentors at Fuller, encouraged me to publish my work.

My research and writing were made easier by the gracious help and support of a number of people. Special gratitude goes to Sue Mosteller, CSJ, the literary executrix of the Henri Nouwen Literary Centre in Canada, for warmly welcoming me during my two visits to L'Arche Daybreak and providing opportunities to conduct interviews with certain key people in Nouwen's life; also for her willingness to read my manuscript and provide insightful feedback. I also want to thank Gabrielle Earnshaw, the archivist of the Henri J. M. Nouwen Archives and Research Collection at the John M. Kelly library of St. Michael's College (University of Toronto) for allowing me access to Nouwen's materials. I am also appreciative of Lowry and Jeanne Chua's incredible hospitality during my visits to Toronto.

Consistent with true Benedictine spirit, Abbot Francis Benedict, OSB; Father Luke Dysinger, OSB; Sister Karen Wilhelmy, CSJ; and Brother Benedict, OSB, made it possible for me to spend extended times at the St. Andrew's Benedictine Abbey in Valyermo. I thank them for their hospitality and for providing me free access to the monastery's library and computer during the early stages of my writing.

Profound gratitude also goes to the following people with whom I had the privilege of discussing Henri Nouwen and my project: Pastor Melvin Fujikawa, Dr. Deirdre LaNoue, John Mogabgab, and Dr. Michael Christensen, whose class on Nouwen, which I attended at Drew University, gave me a boost during the preliminary stages of my research.

Jeff Imbach, president of the Henri Nouwen Society of Canada, read sections of my drafts and gave helpful comments. His course material on Nouwen (offered via correspondence through St. Francis Xavier University) inspired me to design my own course—thanks to my mentor and to Jeannette Scholer, the academic programs director at Fuller, for making this possible. I am indebted to my good friend Jan Johnson, who read major portions of my earlier drafts and gave me invaluable editorial comments. Thanks also to Dr. Michael O' Laughlin for his overall critique of my manuscript.

Finally, to my family: Juliet, my wife, and Jonathan and David, my two teenagers, who all had to adjust many times to my busy writing schedule. Thanks for your patience and understanding. To God who alone deserves all the glory!

Henri J. M. Nouwen's Frequently Cited Works

(ALPHABETICAL LIST WITH CORRESPONDING
ABBREVIATION BY TITLE INITIALS)

Adam: God's Beloved (A)
Behold the Beauty of the Lord (BBL)
Bread for the Journey: A Daybook of Wisdom and Faith (BJ)
Beyond the Mirror: Reflections on Death and Life (BM)
Can You Drink the Cup? (CYD)
Clowning in Rome: Reflections on Solitude, Celibacy, Prayer, and Contemplation (CR)
Compassion (C)
Creative Ministry (CM)
A Cry for Mercy: Prayers from the Genesee (CFM)
The Genesee Diary: Report from a Trappist Monastery (GD)
Finding My Way Home: Pathways to Life and the Spirit (FWH)
¡Gracias! A Latin American Journal (G!)
Heart Speaks to Heart: Three Prayers to Jesus (HSH)
Here and Now: Living in the Spirit (HN)
The Inner Voice of Love: A Journey Through Anguish to Freedom (IVL)
In the Name of Jesus: Reflections on Christian Leadership (INJ)
Intimacy (I)
Letters to Marc About Jesus: Living a Spiritual Life in a Material World (LM)
Life of the Beloved: Spiritual Living in a Secular World (LOB)
Lifesigns: Intimacy, Fecundity, and Ecstasy in Christian Perspective (LS)

The Living Reminder: Service and Prayer in Memory of Jesus Christ (LR)
Making All Things New: An Invitation to the Spiritual Life (MN)
Our Greatest Gift: A Meditation on Death and Dying (GG)
Reaching Out: The Three Movements of the Spiritual Life (RO)
The Return of the Prodigal Son: A Story of Homecoming (RPS)
The Road to Daybreak: A Spiritual Journey (RD)
The Road to Peace (RP)
Sabbatical Journey: The Diary of His Final Year (SJ)
Walk with Jesus: Stations of the Cross (WJ)
The Way of the Heart: Desert Spirituality and Contemporary Ministry (WOH)
With Burning Hearts: A Meditation on the Eucharistic Life (BH)
With Open Hands: Bringing Prayer into Your Life (OH)
The Wounded Healer: Ministry in Contemporary Society (WH)

Introduction

Henri Nouwen and his work continue to generate much interest even after his untimely death in 1996. A steady stream of books, many of which are organized around key themes in Nouwen's life, continue to surface. Most of these, however, come in the form of collections, readers, and devotional materials. Very little work has been done to focus and analyze his unique yet accessible spirituality or his effective approach to spiritual formation.

Overall Thrust

Consequently, the dual focus of this book is the dynamic of Henri Nouwen's spiritual formation and his lived spirituality—two key factors that I believe account for the ongoing spiritual impact of Nouwen.

First, this book presents a holistic approach to spirituality, and one that Henri Nouwen modeled in his ministry of spiritual formation. Nouwen regarded the spiritual journey as integrative—wholly incorporating spirituality, theology, psychology, and ministry in a seamless fashion.

For Henri Nouwen, authentic Christian spirituality was obediently living out the life of God in us through the Spirit of Christa.[1] One fulfills this by cultivating—*inwardly, outwardly,* and *upwardly*—one's relation with *self, others,* and *God.* This threefold dynamic reflects Nouwen's experiential grasp of spirituality's natural link with theology and with psychology as well as its direct correlation to ministry. For Nouwen, all these four key arenas—*spirituality, psychology, ministry,* and *theology*—commingle with one another in dynamic reciprocity.

In his book *Reaching Out*,[2] Henri Nouwen lays out concisely his own schematic vision of our life in the Spirit. Without expounding on the actual contents of this particular book, I utilize Nouwen's concept of the threefold movement of the spiritual life as my own starting point to unravel the interlocking relationships of psychology, ministry, and theology with spirituality.

Thus, this work shows how, on one hand, the *inward* journey to one's innermost self underscores the inevitable intersection between psychology and spirituality. On the other hand, the *outward* movement toward our fellow human beings stresses the invariable connection that exists between spirituality and ministry. Finally, and most importantly, the *upward* movement to reach up to God serves to highlight the inextricable connection of theology and spirituality. Such interrelationships represent what I call a coinherence[3]—that is, a "full and mutual sharing of one thing in the complete reality of the other"—referring to entities that are distinct yet inseparable from each other. This coinherence involving spirituality, psychology, ministry, and theology was precisely what framed Henri Nouwen's holistic and integrated approach to spiritual formation.

Second, this book explores a unique type of spirituality that is decidedly counterintuitive and countercultural. It is about a *spirituality of imperfection*—one that Henri Nouwen himself exemplified throughout his journeying experience. Nouwen keenly recognized the spiritual journey to perfection as a journey through imperfection, along with the realities of struggle, weakness, and incompleteness. The concept itself runs counter to the prevailing cultural ideals of instant progress, quick fix, self-empowerment and actualization, including the inordinate drive of many toward some calculated sense of wholeness.

Henri Nouwen was all about integration. I submit, however, that his pursuit of it was simultaneously driven and tempered by a wide-open recognition of the sobering existence of imperfection. His movement toward integration was imbued with his own spirituality of imperfection.

For Nouwen, spirituality does integrate with psychology (the *inward* movement to the innermost self) but it is a *psychology* of imperfection—wherein the path to increasing wholeness involves the psychological realities of brokenness and woundedness.

Similarly, spirituality integrates with ministry (the *outward* movement toward others) but it is one characterized by a *ministry* of imperfection—where the key to a truly powerful and fruitful ministry is unlocked through the exercise of powerlessness and weakness. Lastly, spirituality integrates with theology (the *upward* movement to God) but it is, nonetheless, represented by a *theology* of imperfection in which the route toward progressive holiness and union with God is paved with struggle and suffering as an important prelude to glory.

Central to the objective of this study is the portrayal of Henri Nouwen as a perfect example of a spirituality of imperfection. It highlights the process by which he embarked upon the spiritual journey himself, however imperfectly: journeying into the depths of his inner self via solitude, reaching out to others through service, and above all, earnestly seeking God in prayer.

In so doing, Henri Nouwen, through the transparent example of his own experience, stands as proof that the journey is far from smooth. The process is riddled with imperfection along the way. As a restless seeker, wounded healer, and faithful struggler, Henri Nouwen emerges as the embodiment of an authentic spirituality lodged in an imperfect personality.

Henri Nouwen's Relevance

With the renewed interest in the inner life of the soul, *spiritual formation* and *soul care* have become the combined terms of preference for many. Directly or indirectly, they point to the natural convergence of spirituality, theology, psychology, and ministry that Henri Nouwen espoused.

As a Dutch Roman Catholic priest who broke into the shifting religious-cultural climate of North America in the mid-1960s with his rare combination of spiritual, theological, psychological, and ministerial insights, Nouwen challenged the impulses and intuitions of the prevailing culture—and the Christian churches it has affected. More pointedly, he reoriented Christians—and continues to do so today—to a more realistic view of the spiritual life and its formation.

Overall, this work endeavors to show how one imperfect saint continues to influence the spiritual climate of North America and beyond in ways that are not only cross-denominational and broadly ecumenical, but even more significantly, countercultural. Indeed, Henri Nouwen's teachings continue to arrest many of the spiritual, psychological, ministerial, and theological distortions adhered to by many Christians—distortions that are continually being fueled by the reigning cultural norms.

The Big Picture

Part 1 explores the integrated nature of our journey. The first three chapters pattern themselves after the three movements of the spiritual life as outlined in Henri Nouwen's book *Reaching Out*, consisting of an *inward* (self), an *outward* (others), and an *upward* (God) thrust. The three movements correspond with the specific constructs of *psychology*, *ministry*, and *theology*, respectively, which are each elaborated on consecutively in these chapters.

Chapter 1 focuses on the inward movement of the spiritual life. As an important preliminary, it surveys the therapeutic alliance between the distinct realms of *psychology* and spirituality, and launches into the discussion of key integration issues and attempts, the dangers and concerns as well as the potentials and prospects related to this growing merger. All these ideas combined together form the background for introducing Nouwen's conceptual approach to spiritual formation.

Chapter 2 is about the journey outward. It examines the vital link between spirituality and *ministry*. Furthermore, it underscores the needful balance between the "interiority" and "exteriority" of one's lived experience—the kind Henri Nouwen himself demonstrated in dialectical tension throughout his life and ministry.

Chapter 3 rounds off the trilogy by highlighting its upward or Godward focus. In particular, it deals with the indivisible relationship between *theology* and spirituality as well as the importance of subscribing to a practical theology of one's lived spirituality just as Nouwen espoused and tried his best to live out.

Part 2 shifts the discussion from the integrated to the imperfect nature of the journey. Basically it shows how the movement toward integration and the journey of imperfection can coexist side by side.

Chapter 4 builds a case for a spirituality of imperfection by establishing biblical-theological foundations, which substantiate the claim that the inward, outward, and upward journey to perfection is through imperfection.

Chapter 5 portrays Henri Nouwen as a perfect example of imperfection via his experiences of being a restless seeker, a wounded healer, and a faithful struggler.

In the conclusion we return to the dual focal points of this book—the dynamic of Henri Nouwen's spiritual formation and his lived spirituality. We see these by distilling his conceptual approach of integration and correlating it directly with his spirituality, which is far from perfect. Henri Nouwen's ongoing spiritual impact on our present time is clearly justified and worthwhile.

PART I

The Integrated *Journey*

"In my end is my beginning."
(T. S. Eliot, "East Coker")

"All is one: the heart of God,
the hearts of all people, our own hearts."
(Henri Nouwen, *Sabbatical Journey*)

"I press on toward the goal...."
(Phil 3:12a)

CHAPTER ONE

Journey Inward

A Brewing Alliance

A new kind of phenomenon began ushering its way in during the 1950s, one that was destined to define the prevailing ethos of American culture for many years. Dubbed the "therapeutic revolution," it started gathering momentum in the mid-sixties and reached its peak in the 1970s through the late 1980s, such that even the domain of religion began donning a more psychological garb.[1]

Around the same time, a marked shift also began taking place in the religious arena—from what sociologist Robert Wuthnow terms "a spirituality of dwelling" to "a spirituality of seeking."[2] While this "seeker-oriented" spirituality was seemingly overtaking the more institutionalized and established form of religion, it was also becoming a coexistent ally of psychology—thriving simultaneously in the therapeutic soil and climate of the period.

It was in the mid-1960s, during the early stages of this brewing alliance between psychology and spirituality that Henri Nouwen first surfaced on the American scene. His influential presence slowly gained a foothold in the early part of the 1970s. As a newly trained psychologist and theologian with a concern for melding psychology and theology, Nouwen's cultural timing could not have been better. Within the religious landscape of America, Henri Nouwen, without question, already had an eager audience waiting anxiously—a receptive generation hungry for the spiritual and well-accustomed to viewing life through psychological lenses.[3]

Henri Nouwen was a firsthand witness to the budding relationship of psychology with spirituality, treating them as complementary. The way he expressed his understanding of their comple-mentary nature, however—specifically as applied to ministry—did evolve over time in keeping with both his changing convic-tions and the changing times. As most of his works reveal, Nouwen's conceptual and practical style of ministry in general and of spiritual formation in particular goes beyond, and at times directly against, the grain of most contemporary versions of psy-chology and spirituality being espoused by many.

This chapter wades through the broad fields of psychology and spirituality and shows Henri Nouwen's sophisticated and nuanced understanding of their complex interrelationship—conceptually, methodologically, and experientially. In his vivid portrayal of Nouwen, biographer Michael Ford brings to the fore Nouwen's instinctive ability to integrate the psychological with the spiritual: "Trained in psychology and steeped in the riches of Christian spirituality, Nouwen managed to balance his awareness of the dynamics of the human psyche with his openness to the workings of the Spirit."[4]

Through Nouwen's embodied example, we shall see not only how psychology intersects with spirituality, but also how a good grasp of their coinherent relationship can impact the way the min-istry of spiritual formation is effectively carried out. But we need to explore first the natural dynamics between psychology and spirituality for us to more sensibly correlate them both into our thinking.

Psychology's Interface with Spirituality

"The revival of spirituality," practical theologian Gerben Heitink avers, "points to 'fundamental deficiencies' in contempo-rary culture, as is apparent from such themes as 'wholeness, inte-gration, meaning-providing frameworks, community, and personal identity'"[5]—themes that bear striking connections with the domain of psychology. That said, it would appear that the current surging wave of spirituality does overlap with the shifting tide of psychology in a lot of intriguing ways.

One popular psychologist who has surveyed broadly the cur-rent spiritual landscape asserts that much of what passes off as contemporary spirituality is nothing but an offshoot of modern psychology.[6] There may be a considerable weight of truth lodged in that observation. Whatever the case may be, there is no mistaking the interface between the two fields is reviving in an ever-increasing measure these days. From the observant eyes of some Christian psychologists, "The swirling winds of postmodernism have created the possibility of using spirituality and psychology in the same sentence."[7]

More recent developments aside, the concepts of soul, spirit, and faith have all been historically construed as constitutive of early psychology before religion and psychology split into opposing paradigms. The truth is that "psychology and religion may be separate entities, yet they share blurred boundaries."[8] After all, both embody lived experiences that incorporate psychological functioning, making their fusion not merely logical but absolutely necessary.[9]

Still, there was a time when Christianity and psychology were viewed as arch rivals—diametrically opposed to each other and locked in a state of perpetual conflict. It was amidst this prevailing environment that Henri Nouwen, shortly after being ordained to the priesthood in 1957, made the unusually bold request from his archbishop in Holland to study psychology. Much to Nouwen's delight, this request was granted without the usually predictable opposition. Nouwen had an intuitive sense, very early on, that the discipline of psychology could well serve as an important ally of pastoral theology. After six long years of concentrated studies in psychology at the University of Nijmegen, Nouwen, on the advice of renowned Harvard psychologist Dr. Gordon Allport, applied and was accepted as a fellow at the Menninger Clinic in Topeka, Kansas—famous for being the birthplace of pastoral psychology and the program for clinical pastoral education (CPE).

By the time Nouwen arrived in the United States in 1964, the field was already ripe for a more spirited conversation about the relationship between psychiatry and religion as well as the integration of psychology and theology.[10] Not coincidentally, the less than cordial relationship between psychology and spirituality—once plagued by mutual suspicion—would soon be characterized increasingly by reciprocal accommodation.

Evidence of this kind of accommodation abounds even today. Indeed, now it is no longer rare to find professionals from both camps who recognize the need for rigorous study of the relationship between Christianity and psychology as a legitimate pursuit. Many Christian counselors testify to the immense benefits they derive from seriously studying psychology. Openly they acknowledge that selective insights from psychology can be relied upon to deepen the work of soul care. Similarly, many psychotherapists nowadays exhibit less qualms in drawing upon the wisdom and resources of spirituality and applying them without apology to their professional practice.[11]

Theologians, too, are adopting a posture of greater openness to the potential of psychology to contribute legitimately toward doing constructive theology.[12] The current relationship between psychology and spirituality can be likened to an interactive loop even as they inform and influence each other in greater ways. Together, psychology and spirituality continue to forge their complementary relationship.

Henri Nouwen himself recognized with clarity this inherent link between psychology and theology, and he, like many others in the pastoral theology movement of his day, consciously tried to hold both of them in dialectical tension.[13] Within his own experience of ministry, however, Nouwen was only too careful not to allow his passion for psychology to drown his fervor for spirituality. He stood convinced that "spiritual dynamics cannot be reduced to...psychological dynamics."[14]

While remaining appreciative of the numerous insights psychology has offered to the work of pastoral ministry in general, Nouwen was also keenly aware of the danger for Christian spirituality to be unwittingly overpowered by psychology. He knew psychology's limitations and he was not one to allow the biblical language to be replaced with a psychological one.[15] From an epistemological standpoint, Nouwen never considered psychology and spirituality on the same plane, even though he regarded them as mutual partners. "What I want to do," Nouwen specified, "is to show and make available the light of the Spirit, which is not necessarily the same or bound to the psychological life, although there are endless interconnections."[16]

With this in view, Nouwen kept urging Christian ministers to pay closer attention to the spiritual dimension of soul care amidst their effort to glean additional insights from the fields of social and behavioral sciences, including psychology. Despite the fact that new modes of caring embodied in contemporary psychologies have proven to be enriching resources for the church, Nouwen maintained that Christians in the helping profession need continually to reclaim the care and cure of souls as primarily a spiritual undertaking.[17] After all, the ministry of healing once stood as an exclusive domain that characterized the mission and mandate of the church before it evolved into a more collaborative and sometimes overlapping task between pastors and psychotherapists.[18] For much of the history of the church, the pastor has been viewed as a curate—a "physician of the soul."[19]

In what appeared to be a calculated move on his part, Henri Nouwen strategically positioned himself with the shifting emphases of the times—from clinical psychology to pastoral psychology to pastoral theology and practical ministry, and into Christian spirituality—without ever invalidating his reputation as a wise integrator of psychology and spirituality in his unique way.[20] Integration remained uppermost throughout his ministry practice.

Psychology's Integration with Spirituality

Given the expansive ways in which psychology and spirituality are interlaced, it comes as no surprise that experts from both fields explore all avenues to better understand and define the relationship of each field with the other. The mounting alliance between them only provides grist for Christian thinkers to continue wrestling with the complex dynamics involved between their firmly held Christian beliefs and the provocative findings of psychology in general.

As a consequent move toward tightening the already established link between spirituality and psychology, a number of experts have advanced countless models of integration, each with a uniquely different slant that at times appear antithetical to one another.[21] Most such efforts, to be sure, are sensible if not substantial exploratory studies, though some perhaps do not hold up to rigorous scrutiny, conceptually as well as methodologically.

The most popular of these various attempts to establish the link between spirituality and psychology is the "integration" model, which itself consists of a host of variations. The reality is, the existing literature in this field has become a bit dizzying—too vast to even start categorizing.

If only to highlight Henri Nouwen's inherent capacity for integration, I introduce at this point three of the current integration concepts whose basic philosophical and methodological features Nouwen no doubt appropriated in his life and ministry. I refer to the *intrapersonal, intradisciplinary,* and *interdisciplinary approaches,* which I will now briefly describe and then illustrate through Nouwen's way of embodying each of them.

Intrapersonal Integration

This kind of integration deals with the integrator's ability to integrate his or her spiritual and psychological experiences in complete consonance with the realities of his or her faith professions and expressions.[22] Of paramount importance is the character of the integrator, that is to say, the person's lived spirituality—which naturally encompasses the entire arena of one's existence. Intrapersonal integration actually stands as the most foundational aspect of integration, "without which, true, biblical integration of psychology and Christianity in the conceptual-theoretical, research, and professional categories cannot be substantially achieved."[23]

Henri Nouwen evidenced this practice of integration through what he himself considered to be his secret journal, *The Inner Voice of Love.* Representing the most personal account of his inward journey, Nouwen demonstrated with characteristic transparency his masterful ability to weave his spiritual and psychological experiences with exceptional rawness and candor. In the thick of excruciating anguish triggered by the sudden interruption of a friendship that meant the world to him, Nouwen did not allow himself to disintegrate as a person despite suffering a nervous breakdown. In Nouwen the spiritual and the psychological were existentially one piece, wholly integrated in both his experience of struggle and eventual liberation. Through his *intrapersonal* processing of reality as he experienced and documented it, we the readers are privileged to catch a deep sense of Nouwen's abiding faith. Consequently we are lent his hope should we find ourselves engaging in similar fierce struggles of our own.[24]

Intradisciplinary Integration

For this second type of integration, the greater thrust of the question is not so much how we ought to understand the relationship between psychology and theology, but how we can use the Christian faith in a practical way during any process of intervention itself—whether it be counseling or therapy. It is this pinpointed concern that has given impetus to the emerging frontier of intradisciplinary integration.[25]

Essentially, such integration involves the construction of a Christian theory of therapeutic or counseling ministry that integrates an individual's faith and practice.[26] The integrative task requires competence beyond the theological and psychological. An experiential understanding of spirituality and the process of spiritual formation are critical if religious issues are to be brought down from the theoretical level into the actual counseling practice.[27]

Once again, we find in Henri Nouwen a luminous example of how intradisciplinary integration works itself out within the actual context of ministering to people. His book *Letters to Marc* witnesses to his seemingly effortless ability to do this type of integration as only a seasoned teacher, guide, and mentor can do. In this insightful collection of letters addressed to his nineteen-year-old nephew, Marc, the practicality of Nouwen's Christ-centered faith and its relevant application to daily existence was employed to great effect as he engaged in an epistolary mode of counseling. With fully charged conviction, Nouwen shared his insights with Marc about life's meaning and direction by explaining to this confused teenager what spiritual living is about: "Living spiritually...concerns the core of your humanity. It is possible to lead a very wholesome, emotionally rich, and 'sensible' life without being a spiritual person: that is, without knowledge or personal experience of the terrain where the meaning and goal of our human existence are hidden."[28] Nouwen was forthright about his intent: he wanted to offer Marc, as he states: "a taste of the richness of life as a Christian as I know it, experience it, and continue to discover it." (*LM*:6)

Interdisciplinary Integration

This last conceptual approach is ably tackled by Deborah van Deusen Hunsinger in her groundbreaking book, *Theology and Pastoral Counseling.*[29] The title carries a definitive tagline: *A New Interdisciplinary Approach*—aimed at underlining a truly unique proposal that in some ways signifies a major departure from the traditional idea of integration most are accustomed to.

Here, Hunsinger's specific tack is to correlate, both clinically and theologically, the widely divergent views of psychologist Carl Jung and theologian Karl Barth. In her work, Hunsinger argues that the effective practice of pastoral counseling demands a combination of psychological and theological expertise on the part of the counselor: He or she must be adept at speaking two distinct languages—one containing the vocabulary of faith and the other the vocabulary of psychology. In other words, pastoral counselors—and everyone in the business of ministering to people—need to acquire bilingual proficiency without necessarily integrating theology and psychology into a single, unified whole as some are wont to do. Theology need not become psychological nor psychology become theological.

Such wide-open opportunity for interdisciplinary integration is something that Henri Nouwen learned to seize early on. Kyle Henderson, in his dissertation on Henri Nouwen, shows how, through the gradual transformation of pastoral theology in the 1990s, Nouwen himself took full advantage of what has come to be known then as "pastoral bilingualism"—akin to Hunsinger's notion of bilingual proficiency.[30]

That Nouwen proved at ease invoking both languages of faith and psychology in an *interdisciplinary* fashion can be attributed in large part to his wealth of concurrent experiences as a trained psychologist and theologian. Nouwen's combined expertise in both arenas is displayed eloquently in his multitopical yet well-unified book *Intimacy,* where we glimpse Nouwen intuitively switching back and forth between pastoral and therapeutic tones with remarkable deftness.[31] Capitalizing on the book's overall theme of intimacy, together with its focus on the inner life of the soul, Henri Nouwen managed to convey his ideas with such bilingual proficiency without the usual technical baggage attached to them.

The above examples show how Henri Nouwen naturally employed *intrapersonal, intradisciplinary,* and *interdisciplinary* integration. These three integration concepts stand out as foundational in the face of all the massive integration efforts being pursued by so many, which at times register as rather forced, if not artificial. Occupying a much broader base in terms of application to real-life ministry, they are the embodiment of practical integration.

Suffice it to say, Henri Nouwen is all about integration—integration of the most practical sort. With a seeming ability to foresee what was ahead of him, Nouwen demonstrated acquaintance with the prospects and potentialities of the growing merger between spirituality and psychology. At the same time he was not naïve about its dangers. Henri Nouwen is reminiscent of the Old Testament tribe of Issachar, "who had understanding of the times" (1 Chr 12:32). As a discerning person, Nouwen evidently knew how to swim in the direction of the current as well as against it. He read and interpreted the times wisely—both the promise and the peril.

Spirituality and Psychology: Promise and Peril

One noteworthy evolvement linked to the escalating popular interest in spirituality and psychology has to do with the varying expressions of rediscoveries made by postmoderns.[32] Two in particular apply directly to our present concern: a reemergence of interest in the soul and a renewed focus on the inner life.

Spirituality and the Soul

Dallas Willard, a philosophy professor known for his spiritual writings, observes: "Practices and concepts that have had a long life in the Christian past are being experienced and explored anew, and many involved in the field of psychology are taking professional interest in them and the soul."[33] As proof of this fascinating rediscovery, we find ourselves nowadays inundated by scores of published works with the word "soul" figuring prominently in their titles.[34] Most represent writings that address the broad subject of soul within the equally broad sphere of spirituality. In the same way that the vocabulary of spirituality has come into vogue, so has the language of the soul.

Despite major disagreements over the concept of the soul, it remains arguably a focal point of interest as it relates to the whole gamut of spirituality. From one psychologist's perspective, there is not even a question that "[t]he whole new spirituality movement is about the soul."[35] Martin Marty, distinguished Professor Emeritus at the University of Chicago, was once asked if he felt the modern soul fascination was authentic, and he replied: "The hunger is always authentic; it's just that you can feed it with Twinkies or with broccoli."[36]

Soul search indeed is a present reality; soul formation is an altogether different matter, particularly if it assumes a more explicit Christian identity. As it is lived out, Christian spirituality concerns the formation of our soul—"reforming the broken soul of [our] humanity in a recovery from its alienation from God"[37]— which encompasses our entire being. It is in this broad sense that spirituality and the soul go together, for Christian spirituality actively engages the soul in its ongoing process of self-renovation: soul making, soul crafting, soul shaping, soul keeping.[38]

Spirituality and the Self

Pollster George Gallup remarked that instead of focusing on outer space, the people's preoccupation on the first decades of the twenty-first century may well be on inner space.[39] The subject of interiority is indeed fast becoming a new fascination for many. According to Robert Wuthnow, hailed as America's leading sociological interpreter of religion, who follows with interest the growing affinity between spirituality and the self, such fascination rings true in light of the inordinate interest people have in the inner self as a way of connecting with the sacred.[40] Henri Nouwen himself thought that "the turn to a spirituality means that many believe in the possibility to know and to experience the inner life" and that "the personal nature of the inner life has been the good condition for the rich and very varied blossoming which makes the spiritual side of the human history so fascinating."[41]

If we agree that spiritual formation is essentially about the formation of the entire human self with its intersecting spiritual and psychological embodiments, its processes "require precise, testable, thorough knowledge of the human self,"[42] according to Dallas Willard. In reality, broad differences continue to exist in the way Christian psychologists and theologians themselves understand and articulate the whole concept of the "self." Thus in approaching this complex matter, we need not be too dogmatic. We are better off if we stay open and perhaps even tentative about our theological as well as psychological positions about it.

The "Self" in Varying Perspectives

At the risk of oversimplification, Christians generally tend to view the self in the extreme: either in the positive or in the negative, as problem or as answer.[43] On the negative side, most people's construal of the self indicates an inordinate focus inward. Despite certain claims to the contrary, many Americans remain immersed in a highly narcissistic culture in which self is enthroned above all else. As is now more apparent than before, our everyday vocabulary is peppered with endless jargon that begins with the prefix "self": self-discovery, self-fulfillment, self-actualization, and so on. The self has become not just our main focus but practically our ultimate obsession. We commonly refer to a "lost self" that needs to be rediscovered; an "empty or deprived self" that has to be filled, fulfilled, realized, and actualized; or even a "bruised, broken, victimized, and wounded self" that demands recovery, healing, and wholeness.

Such a "frantic search for selfhood" through "a self-acquired identity," Henri Nouwen unmasks, is but illusory.[44] Worse, this type of overly self-directed, inward mood, according to Jeffrey Hadden, "seems unbridled by any social norm or tradition and almost void of notions for exercise of responsibility toward others."[45] In short, it smacks of massive self-absorption. Psychologist Paul Vitz labels this so-called cult of self as "selfism," and charges such obsessive inward proclivity as outright idolatry,[46] a tendency that finds subtle expressions in today's differing versions of psychology and spirituality. It is not inaccurate to say that much of contemporary spirituality focuses narrowly on the individual.

Within the field of Christian counseling there exists a tension as to how the notion of "self" ought to be properly addressed. On the one hand, certain Christian counselors, most notably Jay Adams, extol the value of denying and losing oneself (while at the same time vigorously attacking the concepts of "self-esteem" and "self-worth" as unbiblical). On the other hand, others, like Ray Anderson, insist that only a positive concept of the self can take responsibility for being guilty of sin in a healthy way. Anderson argues persuasively that the self remains in the "image" of God and retains its self-identity through God's grace and love. The recovery of this self, Anderson adds, is what is promised in the Gospel.[47] Henri Nouwen declares that from God's perspective, our true identity as his children is one that is defined by himself and is hidden in the center of our being from where we must live.[48]

The Self or Soul and Inwardness

To many, the concept of interiority conjures up overlapping images of both the *self* and the *soul*. Indeed, it is difficult to make a rigid distinction between these two terms. Often they are used interchangeably. James Beck indicates that the "self" has filled in the vacuum left a century ago by the loss of "soul" in psychology.[49] "[W]hat in modern times came to be designated the *self* was known as the *soul*" in an era "when anthropological discussions took their cue from…a wider theological reflection on the meaning of human personhood," Stanley Grenz explained.[50] With the resurgence of "soul" within the standard vocabulary of contemporary society, "self" has come to be used "to bear some of the meaning that soul used to carry."[51]

As stated earlier, the subject of the self, along with its emphasis on interiority, continues to raise some thorny issues over which many Christians, particularly theologians and psychologists, continue to be divided. Here is one area where theology and psychology undeniably intersect and where a dialogue, if not a serious effort at correlation between the two disciplines, is most warranted.

For the most part, the present notion of "self," like "soul," focuses on inwardness or interiority.[52] This similar focus, which has characterized much of the mystical tradition of the past, has become a familiar construct which, for better or for worse, is now generally associated with the main province of psychology.

Without a doubt, inwardness does constitute a psychological movement. After all, psychology is unavoidably a self-reflective task.[53] That is not to claim though that the interior journey is purely and exclusively a psychological enterprise.

Henri Nouwen is said to have similarly embarked on an inward psychological journey himself—moving to self-awareness in an existentialist sense without necessarily being self-absorbed. This Nouwen did without framing his experience in strictly psychological terms even though it contained psychological underpinning.[54]

Psychology: A Journey Inward

Henri Nouwen considered the matrix of psychology beneficial insofar as it aids us in the understanding of "self" in relation to God. To Nouwen, self-knowledge is integral to the development of the spiritual life. Knowing our self does pave the way for us to get in touch with our inner core. "As people on an inward journey," Elizabeth O'Connor reminds us, "...we are committed to growing in consciousness, to becoming people in touch with our real selves, so that we know not only what flows at the surface, but what goes on *in the depths of us*" (emphasis mine).[55] This deep part of us is what Henri Nouwen called the inner sanctuary of our being,[56] where God chooses to reach in and dwell. Calvin Miller echoes it this way: "*Deep* is the dwelling place of God."[57]

Many of us can testify to times when we experience God's very presence permeating through our depths. It is as though a mysterious light shines within. An inner light awakens us to our true self and causes change to occur from the inside. Profound God-awareness can lead to self-awareness; deep self-awareness can lead to real conversion. That massive self-awareness can drive one to repentance is strikingly portrayed in Nouwen's own retelling of the familiar story of the prodigal son. Nouwen recounts how a complete sense of feeling lost awakened the son to his senses, which eventually led him to the "rediscovery of his deepest self" and forced him to confront "the bottom line of his identity" (*RPS*:48–49). It is this quality of inner transformation that brings about true integration within a person—a deep sense of integrity.[58]

This deep experience of ourselves captures the nature of our inward journey. Henri Nouwen himself embarked on what journalist Philip Yancey calls a form of "inward mobility" wherein "[h]e withdrew in order to look inward, to learn how to love God and be loved by God."[59] Such movement is best realized in the context of solitude. In solitude, we can pay closer attention to our inner self and consequently become present to our own experience (*RO*:41). Our inward ability to relate to and be at home with our own self is what enables us to live life from the center of our existence and thereby relate with others in terms of who we are and not so much by what we do (*I*:149). Reaching into our inmost being connects us to the reality of our own soul—that mystical reality that Henri Nouwen simply calls the *heart*.

What other scholars tend to distinguish as "soul," "self," "spirit," or "will," Nouwen preferred to lump together in his uncluttered thinking as the "heart." In more ways than one, Nouwen's focus on the heart symbolizes best the essence of his spirituality where life is lived from the core of one's being—that "space within us where God dwells and we are invited to dwell with God."[60]

Lamentably, Nouwen confessed, it is also from this "hidden center" that "we are most alienated from ourselves...strangers in our own house" (*LM*:74). The challenge, therefore, is for us to connect deeply with our own hearts and there discover who we really are. The inward journey, then, as it was for Nouwen, is a heart-centered movement into one's innermost self—a journey of self-discovery toward wholeness.

Psychology's Coinherence with Spirituality

The inward journey toward the self, which was for Henri Nouwen, as it is for us, the *sine qua non* for self-knowledge, is a journey well worth taking. For one thing, it is not a solitary journey since the self necessarily intersects with the Divine.

No other person in Christian history has so eloquently described the nature of this interior experience than Augustine, one of the most revered saints of the Western church. With his view of the introspective conscience, Augustine stands out as one of the very first Christian thinkers to articulate a psychological understanding of the soul or self or heart that is consonant with the knowledge of the triune God.[61] His articulation is so profound that it recalibrates our focus more clearly toward the coinherent nature of the relationship between psychology and spirituality, which involves knowing self and knowing God.

Knowing Self, Knowing God

"I want to know God and the soul" sums up Augustine's opening prayer in his famous *Soliloquies*.[62] It is clear from this prayer that Augustine's passionate desire reflected an eager readiness "to find [his] selfhood in the longing for communion with an eternal 'other.'"[63] For Augustine, the knowledge of self is the first step toward the soul's knowledge of God.[64] As Henri Nouwen put it very directly: "You cannot know God if you don't even know who you are."[65]

In the opening section of *The Institutes of the Christian Religion,* John Calvin introduced the concept of "double knowledge": "...true and sound wisdom, consists of two parts: the knowledge of God and of ourselves."[66] Calvin was explicit that these two forms of knowledge are virtually inseparable. Many other spiritual thinkers agree.

The contemplative Trappist monk Thomas Merton likens the spiritual life to "a journey in which we discover ourselves in discovering God, and discover God in discovering our true self hidden in God."[67] Søren Kierkegaard could thus assert: "The more conception of God, the more self; the more self, the more conception of God."[68]

The way Henri Nouwen (whom author Ronald Rolheiser called "our generation's Kierkegaard"[69]) perceived the crucial connection is that "we become strangers to ourselves" the more we act as strangers before God.[70] The kind of intimacy that Nouwen yearned to experience, which he believed God offers us, is one in which "we can be most ourselves when most like God."[71] Nouwen further affirms to himself: "I am hidden in God and I have to find myself in that relationship."[72] Thus for Nouwen, as for Kierkegaard, the self ultimately derives its meaning in relation to God. Nouwen exhibits a firm handle on the reciprocal dynamic of knowing self and knowing God.

Henri Nouwen's own grasp of what Calvin referred to as "double knowledge" definitely goes beyond the theoretical realm; he had his experience to back up his understanding. In reading *The Genesee Diary* (Nouwen's intensely personal journal, which chronicles in detail his seven-month experience in a Trappist monastery), one can sense his evident "growth in self-knowledge and God-knowledge" that not only proved so heart-transforming for him, but also brought about greater coherence and integrity to his whole journeying experience.[73]

David Benner is right: "...an understanding of Christian spirituality that affirms the interdependence of the deep knowing of God and self...integrates us in our depths and makes us both whole and holy."[74]

Unity of Soul and Spirit

More and more people involved in providing soul care seem to exhibit a growing understanding of and deeper appreciation for the practical ramifications of the interconnectedness between the enigmatic concepts of spirit and soul. Instinctively many can recognize that the soul and the spirit are somewhat united.

David Benner, in particular, believes that the soul represents the meeting place of the psychological and the spiritual. According to him, a correct understanding of the nature of the soul "reunites the psychological and the spiritual and directs the activities of those who care for the souls of others in such a way that their care touches the deepest levels of people's inner lives." Additionally, he points out, "The spiritual quest is, at one level, a psychological quest, and every psychological quest can be understood to be in some way reflective of our basic spiritual quest." Therefore, strictly speaking, it logically follows that "[n]o problem of the inner person is either spiritual or psychological; all problems are psychospiritual."[75] To insist otherwise is a false dichotomy.

Psychospiritual unity does highlight the crucial interrelatedness of the spiritual and psychological spheres of human personality. Moreover, it substantiates the coinherent status of psychology and spirituality.

Conclusion

Psychology and spirituality, though distinctly separate fields, do reciprocally influence each other by virtue of the unity of personhood. In all likelihood, we may not be able to grasp accurately the dynamics between them any more than we can crystallize in our perception the complex interaction between the soul (psyche) and spirit (pneuma). It is sufficient enough to know that the two worlds constantly interpenetrate and consequently influence each other, especially within one's own experience.

Psychology and spirituality are invariably linked just as the reality of the soul and the spirit are dynamically interconnected in one's being. Inevitably, the interior journey of the soul intersects with spiritual reality where self-discovery ushers one into God-discovery and vice-versa. Our search for wholeness simply cannot be divorced from our movement toward holiness since the knowledge of God and the knowledge of the self are always bound to commingle in every Christian's inward journey experience.

Henri Nouwen seemed to exhibit an intuitive understanding of this profound dynamic at work. He evidently lived out this existential reality himself. Nouwen's heart-centered approach to spirituality brings to a unified focus our joint pursuit of holiness and wholeness.

Psychology does coinhere with spirituality as far as our inward journey is involved. But also for our outward journey, spirituality coinheres with ministry just as well.

CHAPTER TWO

Journey Outward

Reaching Out

Following Henri Nouwen's threefold movement of the spiritual life—toward self, others, and God—I basically recast the first movement by linking it with the inward journey into our own heart and soul. Drawing upon the rubric of psychology while being guided by the spiritual insights of Nouwen, we homed in on the importance of self-knowledge in connection with our pursuit of wholeness.

We also noted how the knowledge of self inevitably inter-weaves with the knowledge of God. As shown, this "double-knowledge" steers us in the direction toward a more integrated pursuit of wholeness and holiness in our life. On a similar trail, it also projects the coinherent manner in which psychology entwines with spirituality—a reality Henri Nouwen intuitively demonstrated himself.

This particular chapter focuses on the outward movement: *reaching out to others*—with its decided emphasis on ministry. Here I will discuss the equally intertwining relationship between spirituality and ministry based on the Great Commandment (Matt 22:37–39)—to love God and our neighbor. In what follows, I want us to examine closely what I choose to call *a spirituality of ministry* (love of God) and *a ministry of spirituality* (love of others). In the process, we hope to gain a deeper sense of how exactly spirituality and ministry interrelate.

Under these two categories, we will see not only how the key realities of communion and community intersect in Henri Nouwen's experiential understanding of them, but also how the common thread of prayer weaves itself in and through both of them. Specifically for Nouwen, it is our communion with God, on one hand, that provides the solid foundation for our spirituality of ministry. On the other hand, it is the community—of God and of humanity—that gives shape to our ministry of spirituality.

Spirituality of Ministry

Many believers who embark on ministry sooner or later discover that the demands of the task can prove very overwhelming. The question is this: Why is it that not too many people make it over the long haul? One chief condition among many others that perennially afflicts most ministries as well as ministers is what well-known author Eugene Peterson labels as the crisis of "undercapitalized vocation."[1] Many simply do not have what it takes to spiritually fund their ministry undertakings in such a way that they are endowed with staying power. We all are in dire need of an adequate spiritual capital to sustain us throughout our ministry journey.

To not only survive but flourish in the ministry, we must possess a strong spiritual interior able to stand up to the exterior demands of ministry. In short, we need a deep spirituality of ministry that flows continually through our "ministerial veins," so to speak. Henri Nouwen himself nailed it down: Ministry has to be underpinned by spirituality.[2]

Communion: The Foundation of Spirituality

The only "interior" spirituality that can support us through our ongoing process of formation in Christ is that which firmly roots itself in an abiding communion with God. Communion is what being in "union with" means. It involves nourishing the already existing connection we have with God and raising it to an intimate level where we come closest to experiencing what we have been created for: full communion. Indeed, "God has given us a heart that will remain restless until it has found full communion" (*HN*:43).

Only a deeply rooted communion can enable the growth of our character in Christ and consequently empower our service for him. A discernible pattern of spiritual progression emerges out of this perspective: The first emphasis is on intimacy (being with

Christ), followed by formation (becoming like Christ), and lastly, service (living for Christ).[3] This is spiritual formation in a nut-shell—the way Henri Nouwen understood it, lived it, and administered it to others.

Intimacy: Inflow of Communion

Eugene Peterson recognizes by the very nature of spirituality the intrinsic feature of intimacy that lies deep within the core of our being. This reality, he says, intermingles with a profound longing for transcendence in everyone's experience—like a compelling force of the "within" yearning to connect to the "beyond."[4] Henri Nouwen identified this mysterious sense with "the stirrings of the soul" (*I*:149)—a hunger for intimacy and communion with God, who implanted such deep longing inside us all.

We desire intimacy—both we and God—which can only find fruition in mutual communion between God and us. From our end, we need only to learn how to be with Christ so we can experience the reality of God's loving presence. Jesus' invitation to abide in his love as expressed in John 15:10 is, for Nouwen, "an invitation to a total belonging, to full intimacy, to an unlimited being-with."[5]

In the Gospel of Mark we are told that Jesus "appointed twelve...to be *with* him [emphasis mine], and to be sent out to proclaim the message" (Mark 3:14). The application is revealing: Intimacy comes first before ministry—a chronology most of us conveniently reverse by becoming aggressive workers for God first before becoming humble worshipers of God.

In this regard, Mike Yaconnelli issued a confession many of us—if we are honest enough to admit it—can resonate with: "I knew what it meant to believe in Jesus; I did not know what it meant to *be* with Jesus [author's emphasis]....I found it easy to do the work of God, but had no idea how to let God work in me."[6] This seems to be the testimony of many Christians whose idea of experiencing God's presence is too abstract at best, totally unreal at worst.

Formation: Outgrowth of Communion

For Henri Nouwen, nothing could be more real than communing with God at deepening levels, thereby allowing God to progressively transform his character from one increment of glory to a higher one. The apostle Paul, in 2 Corinthians 3:18, graphically pictures this for us: "And all of us, with unveiled faces, seeing the glory of the Lord as though reflected in a mirror, are being transformed into the same image from one degree of glory to another;..."(2 Cor 3:18).

Nouwen believed, with Ignatius of Loyola, in utilizing all of our senses in our contemplation such that as we "imagine the reality of the divine as fully as possible...we can slowly be divinized by that reality."[7] We do become like the person upon whom we concentrate the most. To the degree that we spend time communing with Christ, our character becomes shaped more like him. As our character is gradually formed, so are our inner motivations. Our energies are directed toward living for God. Consequently, serving him in ministry becomes our overriding desire.

Service: Outflow of Communion

Throughout the Gospels, Jesus modeled the utmost priority of his own relationship with his heavenly Father. Henri Nouwen stresses that Jesus' "primary concern was to be obedient to his Father, to live constantly in his presence. Only then did it become clear to him what his task was in relationship with people."[8] Jesus never claimed anything for himself; he always viewed his work as accomplishing the will of God, his Father. The very core of his own ministry lies in his intimate relationship with his Father. In short, Christ's ministry simply flowed out of his deep communion with God.

When asked once by an interviewer about his personal view of spirituality, Henri Nouwen equated it with his concept of the mystical life, which he distinguished from the moral life as a life of communion, intimacy, and belongingness with God.[9] One aspect of this mystical side of communion is described metaphorically by Jesus himself as the connectedness between the vine and its branches. Nouwen interpreted it this way: "In communion with Jesus, the vine, my little life can grow and bear fruit....My true spiritual work is to let myself be loved, fully and completely, and to trust that in that love I will come to the fulfillment of my vocation" (*SJ*:165).[10]

In an unsparing effort to drive home his point, Nouwen reiterated that "[i]f it is true that only with, in and through Jesus Christ can our ministry bear fruits, then our first and only concern must be to live in an ongoing communion with Him who has sent us out to witness in His name."[11] Consequently, it becomes impossible for us not to minister if we maintain solid communion with God and exist within the context of community.

Not only did Nouwen subscribe to the notion that communion generates community because "the God living in us makes us recognize the God in our fellow humans," but that community itself "always leads to mission."[12] Mission, ministry, and service all serve as "the overflow of [our] love for God and for [our] fellow human beings."[13] Clearly, Nouwen allowed no sharp distinction between "the spiritual life from life in community, belonging to God from belonging to each other and seeing Christ from seeing one another in him."[14] To him all these various experiences are woven together into a single spread of spiritual reality.

In summary, we experience a genuine inflow of intimacy by simply being with Christ, constantly deepening our communion with him. The natural outgrowth of such ongoing communion is the increasing formation of our character in Christ. Out of our growing character flows the equally growing conviction to live for Christ in his service.

A final thought: The inflow, outgrowth, and outflow of communion cannot take place apart from the inner dynamic of prayer. Communion and prayer, as Henri Nouwen jointly considered them, represent inseparable facets of the one and the same foundation for our spirituality of ministry.

Communion and Prayer

Prayer, no doubt, occupied a central role in Henri Nouwen's conception of the spiritual life. He not only wrote extensively on the subject of prayer but spoke of it like his own lifeline: "Prayer is the way to let the life-giving Spirit of God penetrate all the corners of my being. Prayer is the divine instrument of my wholeness, unity and inner peace" (*SJ*:5). Spirituality and prayer are likened by Nouwen to the image of spiritual connectedness—which he described as "a way of living united with God" (LR:34).

In Nouwen's vocabulary, prayer and communion are invoked side by side. Prayer has directly to do with one's pursuit to achieve union with God. "To pray is to move to the center of all of life and all love," entering into the depths of one's own heart where God's heart is (HN:23). True prayer involves communing with God, and communion with God involves praying. With his wide-ranging idea of communing prayer, Nouwen incorporated two key practices together: solitude and contemplation.

Prayer and Solitude

We all need a quiet center in which we cultivate our inner freedom to live our life in the Spirit. "Solitude [is] the place of an intimate encounter, the place where we commune with God," revealed Henri Nouwen.[15] Implied here is solitude's partnership with silence as essential to a spirituality of ministry. Without a set aside time and place alone with God, we cannot be adequately formed spiritually, according to Nouwen, for solitude stands for the furnace in which our transformation occurs (MN:69).

Solitude as a discipline serves as one of the most powerful disciplines pertaining to the development of a strong prayer life. As Nouwen validated through his own experience, it is a simple avenue by which we can begin to listen to God's voice in a fresh and new way (MN:75). Nouwen said it well: "...the measure of [our] solitude is the measure of [our] capacity for communion" (GD:48). Indeed, we are well-tuned in to God when we make concentrated time for him.

Prayer and Contemplation

Communing prayer does not only grow out of the place and practice of solitude; it also gets sustained and deepened through the disciplined exercise of contemplation. "Contemplation," Henri Nouwen claimed, "is one of the sure roads to unceasing communion with the Beloved" (CR:74). Contemplation engages our inner capacity to see into and through the center of reality. In contemplative prayer, "we begin to see God in our heart" and allow him to "take possession of all our senses."[16] The process involves "letting [Jesus] enter fully into our consciousness so that he becomes the icon always present in the inner room of our hearts" (*CR*:36).

Authentic prayer, said Nouwen, "makes us into what we imagine" and "leads [us] to becoming like God" (*G!*:30). Communing in prayer and praying in communion transform us inside and out. They both solidify the foundation for our spirituality of ministry and free us to engage actively in our ministry of spirituality.

Ministry of Spirituality

In setting forth the spirituality of ministry, we surfaced three key elements in the dynamics of our spiritual life: intimacy (being with Christ), formation (becoming like Christ), and service (living for Christ) in that order of progression. This same sequence leads us to a working definition of spiritual formation that incorporates both a Godward focus as well as an outward focus toward humanity while deliberately highlighting the ministry side of it: Spiritual formation is the lifelong journey of experiencing the presence of Christ such that we become increasingly formed in his character and are thus enabled to live our lives for his service on behalf of others. A shorter version, in keeping with the threefold schema might be worded like this: Spiritual formation is the process of being with Christ in order to become like Christ and consequently live for Christ. Yet there is a rationale behind the working definition I propose.

While the correct stress on service is integral to the above-mentioned schema, I want to showcase its wider meaning by emphasizing that true spiritual service is directed both to Christ and to others in a mutually inclusive way. When we serve Christ, we actually do so for the benefit of others; too, when we serve others, we are really serving Christ (see Matt 25:35–40). In Henri Nouwen's succinct way of putting it, "...service to the neighbor is also service to God" (*LR*:32). Such an expansive interpretation of service brings into greater focus the ministry thrust that often gets evacuated from other popular notions of spiritual formation.

Henri Nouwen's concept of formation definitely reflects the kind of outward movement that is inherent in the ministry of spirituality. As he expounded on it elsewhere, "Spiritual Formation gives us a free heart able to see the face of God in the midst of a hardened world and allows us to use our skills to make that face visible to all who live in darkness."[17]

Ultimately, the blessing of ministry, Nouwen uncovers, includes the opportunity of glimpsing the face of God in the face of Jesus seen in everyone who needs our care (HN:83). Broadly speaking, the ministry of spirituality centers around the ministry of service to Christ for the full benefit of others.

Community: The Contour of Ministry

What exactly then does this ministry grounded in the Great Commandment look like, particularly the way Henri Nouwen exemplified it? To be sure, one compelling reality that Nouwen could not afford to isolate from the ministry of service is that of the fundamental context of community. To him, community defines the shape of ministry.

Before we proceed, however, with Henri Nouwen's own articulation of the essence of community, it might help to provide a brief sketch of our existing community scenario—which is still in a state of flux. In reality, much of what Nouwen had to say about community connects relevantly with the issues and concerns confronting us today.

Community, in present usage, is a term invested with varied—and at times even contradictory—meanings such that one can easily get lost in the rhetorical maze. The existing communitarian dialogue in religious circles points to the complexity inherent in the shape and texture of the term community as it is appealed to in various contexts.

It is true that our contemporary society, with its unbounded plurality, is woefully lacking integration. Such a scenario is characterized by a heavy sense of displacement and fragmentation.[18] In a paradoxical way, the desire for community appears to be "both developing and dying simultaneously...in the Western world."[19]

Amidst the grim reality of community disintegration comes a fresh yearning for community that is evident in our day. But as one critic notes with dismay, "...[a]s much as we yearn for community, we yearn even more for the social and economic prizes individual mobility can bring."[20] How true that "[d]espite a nostalgia for community, individualism yields slowly to the reawakening of communal sensibilities."[21] What a sad commentary about a gripping cultural reality that exposes the alarming extent to which the malignant disease of individualism has contaminated virtually every aspect of American life! Yet on the brighter side, there are indeed encouraging signs which indicate that we are approaching a period of "social recapitalization," which can productively fund our efforts to "reweave the fabric of communities."[22]

Long before community started occupying a central feature in the rhetoric of our present day, Henri Nouwen had already elevated it as a prominent theme in a number of his writings. The depth and the richness with which he tackled the subject of community still holds enormous applicability to our current situation. Many of Nouwen's countercultural emphases are bound to arrest our sometimes distorted picture of community.

Henri Nouwen's perspective about community is expressly broad, even though his usual starting point is Christian in focus. Conceptually, Nouwen often framed the idea of community foremost in religious or spiritual terms without implying that they are the only legitimate or the normative contexts for invoking its use. In his stated understanding, "Religious community is ecclesia, which means called out of the land of slavery to the free land" (*I*:102). In an important way, this depicts the church, the body of believers who comprise what Nouwen and others generally refer to as the Christian community. Furthermore, this community exists for the deliberate purpose of ministry—a spiritual ministry that is directed and employed *in* community, *by* the entire community, *to* the larger community. To this larger discussion we now turn.

Ministry in Community

Ministry itself is a shared reality whose communal identity bears a definitive character focus—that of compassion rooted in God's compassionate character. The compassionate life, according to Henri Nouwen, is a "life together," "a life in community."[23] The mystery of our new way of being together in compassion has become possible because we have been given a share in God's compassion (C:22). Thus we express our corporate identity as a compassionate community by living out the compassionate character of God before others via the avenue of ministry.

Ministry is never accomplished in detachment from community; ministry is always done within its context. We do ministry *in* community together as a body since community is not only a shared reality but also a shared burden that requires us to act together as one.

Ministry by Community

In one sense, ministry can be viewed as "primarily a vocation given by and performed in the name of the community."[24] In community we can experience transformation that can manifest the presence of God's limitless compassion to the world. It is in this visible expression of compassion "where ministry and spirituality touch each other."[25]

As envisioned by Henri Nouwen, the dynamics of community life in which God's compassion can become more pronounced consist of the paradoxical sense that people are gathered together in voluntary displacement. These two poles, *displacement* and *togetherness*, principally distinguish a mature community existence from a comfortable and protective one associated with mere sentimentalism.

Displacement

God's call to community is a call to move away from our ordinary and comfortable places. Community as the place of compassion requires some measure of displacement to "counteract the tendency to become settled in a false comfort and forget the fundamentally unsettled position that we share with all people" (C:64).

Nouwen sets Jesus as the supreme example of divine displacement via the mystery of the incarnation wherein God chose not to remain in his proper abode but took a humble place by dwelling with humanity through the person of Jesus Christ. In a very real sense, "God displaced himself so that nothing human would be alien to him and he could experience fully the brokenness of our human condition" (C:65). Thus, in Jesus, we see a moving portrait of the displaced Lord "in whom God's compassion becomes flesh" (C:65). Through this striking analogy, Nouwen indirectly challenges us to a lifestyle of discipleship where voluntary displacement is deemed inevitable (C:64).

Togetherness

The other pole in Henri Nouwen's dynamics of community revolves around the notion of togetherness. As Nouwen paradoxically puts it, "The Christian community gathers in displacement and in so doing discovers and proclaims a new way of being together" (C:75). Such a unique sense of togetherness emanates from "a deep sense of being called together to make God's compassion visible in the concreteness of everyday living" (C:76).

In the first place, life in community must be construed as a response to a vocation or to a call since God himself calls us together "into one people fashioned in the image of Christ." Simply put, "It is by Christ's vocation that we are gathered" (C:83), making the Christian community one that is drawn rather than driven together (C:76). The concept of voluntary displacement on which Nouwen anchors his initial emphasis finds its significance only when a gathering together takes place in a new way. Displacement is seen virtually as inauthentic when it does not result in a community being brought closer together.

Ministry to Community

Ministry not only takes place in the context of community and is done as a communal effort; ministry is ultimately aimed toward the community at large. Community is indeed a place of belonging, but Jean Vanier, the Canadian founder of the worldwide communities of L'Arche, sets forth yet another crucial dimension to this so-called notion of community belongingness. In so doing, he helps expand our understanding of belonging by assigning to it the role of "a necessary mediation between an individual and society," functioning as "the fulcrum point for the individual between a sense of self and a sense of society."[26]

Vanier takes belonging as part and parcel of being human and precisely the place to discover what it means to act in a human way. Belonging also happens to be the place that is necessary, in a broader sense, in order to live and act in a pluralistic society.[27] Within this framework, "community life takes on a wider meaning" because "it is lived out not only among its own members, but in the larger community of its neighbourhood, with the poor, and with all those who want to share its hope."[28] Henri Nouwen considers it our necessary calling as a community to keep paying special attention to those who are on the margins of our society.[29] Put more simply, community is inclusive, not exclusive.

Nouwen emphasizes that as members of the Christian community, "we are not primarily for each other but for God," and as such, we are not to be a closed circle of people embracing only one another (RO:154). Our Christian community must take care that it does not, in any way, promote even a semblance of exclusion. We do well to heed Dietrich Bonhoeffer's instructive warning: "The exclusion of the weak and insignificant, the seemingly useless people, from a Christian community may actually mean the exclusion of Christ...."[30]

Scriptures imply that the neighborhood to which we need to reach out in love is ultimately the world. The Great Commandment and the Great Commission (Matt 28:18–20) go together. To love God and others means to reach out to the world that God loves.

How is it then possible for us to reach out to the larger community of the world? Here, Nouwen uncovers the great mystery of the Incarnation: "The closer we come to the heart of God, the closer we come to the heart of the people of God....[W]hen we are in the most intimate corner of our being, we find ourselves most intimately connected with the people of the world."[31] We are placed together so that we can reach out together, although this new togetherness is but the beginning place of compassionate practice (C:82).

True, every community has to have the stability that togetherness brings, but "our destiny is beyond our togetherness" (RO:153). Community likewise needs the mobility that displacement creates for the higher purpose of ministry. Community is therefore cut out for service in the ministry and for the ministry of service.

We can now fathom more clearly how the ministry of spirituality is contoured around the existential reality of community. To start with, Christian spirituality itself is irreducibly communal.

"A life in the Spirit is...a life in community," Henri Nouwen specifies (*BBL*:59). In fact, "apart from a vital relationship with a caring community a vital relationship with Christ is not possible" at all (*C*:61). Indeed, spirituality and community are a joint reality together with ministry—where prayer as "the language of community" (*RO*:156) serves to fuel their shared engine, in a manner of speaking.

Community and Prayer

Henri Nouwen seemed always to breathe out the language of prayer within the environment of community.[32] To him, communal and individual prayer "belong together as two folded hands" (*RO*:158). His firm belief is that one's prayer life cannot exist independent of community life, for prayer "leads to community, and community to prayer."[33]

Nouwen's deep desire was always to form, not just any community, but most specifically, a "prayerful community."[34] It was his conviction that community gets created and expressed, as well as realized in its fullness by means of prayer (*RO*:156). Prayer in the context of community finds concrete outlets through both ministry and service.

Prayer and Ministry

Prayer is socially relevant particularly as it gets directed toward our neighbors.[35] Drawing from experience, Henri Nouwen testifies: "In praying for others, I lose myself and become the other, only to be found by the divine love which holds the whole humanity in a compassionate embrace" (*GD*:144). In the faithful exercise of prayer we discover not only our blessedness, but also our power to bless others through ministering to them.[36]

Prayer cannot and should not be seen as external to the ministry process since "all ministry is based on our personal and communal relationship with God," which finds its ultimate center in the experiential reality of prayer (*LR*:32, 34). Prayer and ministry travel together on the same track and must never be cut off from each other. Prayer itself is ministry and ministry is our prayerful service to God.

Prayer and Service

"Service is prayer and prayer is service" encapsulates the theme of Henri Nouwen's *The Living Reminder*. It ties in with the relationship between our love for God and our love for our neighbor stipulated in the Great Commandment. To love and serve God is to love and serve our neighbor. The way Nouwen explains it, our "unconditional and unreserved love for God" is what "leads to the care of our neighbor," for "[i]t is in God that we find our neighbors and discover our responsibility to them" (*LR*:31–32).

A truly holistic spirituality is one that combines prayer, community, ministry, and service as integral parts of our whole life in God.[37] We, therefore, cannot allow a disconnect in our conception of spirituality and ministry, according to Nouwen's repeated insistence. Prayer emerges as the common thread that runs through our communion with God as well as our community with others. Community in prayer gives shape to the ministry of spirituality.

Service: The Praxis of Ministry

If community in prayer represents the contour of ministry, then what could embody the praxis of ministry from Henri Nouwen's perspective? I believe it boils down to what Henri Nouwen describes so explicitly as compassionate service with solidarity in view.

We are called to respond to human suffering wherever it may be found. However, we first have to experience a sense of inner solidarity with our fellow human beings. It is this deep, personal solidarity that enables us in the first place to feel compassion for others (*RO*:59). In Henri Nouwen's consideration, the contemplation of suffering is bound together with compassion. As a community of compassion, it is critical that we enter into the pains and sufferings of our fellow human beings and be in conscious solidarity with those who live disrupted lives.

Along this line, Nouwen qualifies:

[w]e are not called to respond to generalities but to the concrete facts with which we are confronted day after day. A compassionate man can no longer look at these manifesta-

tions of evil and death as disturbing interruptions of his life plan but rather has to confront them as opportunity for the conversion of himself and his fellow human beings. (*RO*:60)

Nobel Peace Prize recipient Elie Wiesel agrees. From an ethical perspective, he insists, "…it is impossible for human beings…who have seen what people can do to themselves and to one another, not to get involved." A real community that practices solidarity, from his view, is composed of those who want to be with those who suffer, as well as with those who try to prevent others from suffering.[38] A compassionate community aligns itself with others who carry the same burden in order to be more effectively aligned with those who are themselves heavily burdened.

The compassionate life, as Nouwen's own experience bears out, is unlike what most of us are inclined to think it is about. Its focus is on downward mobility, the "downward movement toward solidarity" with "the way of the poor, the suffering, the marginal, the prisoners, the refugees, the lonely, the hungry, the dying, the tortured, the homeless—toward all who ask for compassion" (*HN*:103, 101). In other words, it is the descending way of Jesus through whom we have tasted God's own act of compassion (*C*:27). In and through this same quality of compassion "we can begin to live in solidarity with each other as fully and intimately as God lives with us" (*C*:22).

Communal meaning presupposes the presence of solidarity, especially with justice and equality in view. God's prescribed path toward peace and justice among people is via the road of compassion, which is "to be with others when and where they suffer and to willingly enter into a fellowship of the weak" (*HN*:99).

Nouwen explains perceptively that "[c]ompassion is born when we discover in the center of our own existence not only that God is God and man [*sic*] is man, but also that our neighbor is really our fellow man" (*WH*:41). He invites us to deepen our grasp of it such that it becomes our own personal conviction. What Nouwen wants imbibed in our consciousness is the settled understanding and inner recognition that our neighbor shares our humanity. We can then say with real compassion, "In the face of the oppressed I recognize my own face and in the hands of the oppressor I recognize my own hands" (*OH*:56). Such is true compassionate solidarity.

Another distinct quality of a compassionate community is that of servanthood. As a community, we can transcend our individual limitations and become a concrete realization of the self-emptying way of Christ by our faithful commitment to serve others, especially the needy, the oppressed, the marginalized and disenfranchised.

Here is where the ordering and shaping of communities prove nonnegotiable insofar as the service thrust of community is concerned. The ordering of community not only can give shape to the gifts of its members but it can also provide institutional reliability as "[t]he practice takes on life through...the whole assortment of shared commitments and institutional arrangements that order common life."[39] Author Marva Dawn further enlightens our thinking in this area by pointing out that

> [t]o work and share together more closely as a community is beneficial not merely for its own sake....Beyond that, the results of such sharing would increase the credibility of our message of Christianity. Diversities of gifts offer more possibilities for manifesting the presence of Christ in our midst and for being open to all kinds of people.[40]

Service of Hospitality

One practical way a compassionate community can give solid expression to its members' blended gifts is through the service of hospitality. *Hospitality* is "a practice deeply embedded in the narratives and teachings of the Christian tradition, a practice that recognizes the vulnerability of strangers, the dangers of exclusion, and God's special presence in the guest-host relationship."[41]

Christ himself lays it out for us in no uncertain terms that the real hospitality that is graced with his presence involves ministering to the hungry and thirsty, to the stranger and needy, to the sick and in prison (see Matt 25:35–40). Henri Nouwen may well be right in specifying that the service of hospitality can "offer a new dimension to our understanding of a healing relationship and the formation of a recreative community in a world so visibly suffering from alienation and estrangement" (*RO*:67).

Henri Nouwen views hospitality as a fundamental attitude toward our fellow human beings that can be expressed in several different ways. In his book *Reaching Out*, Nouwen creatively applies hospitality to what he calls the "ins" and "outs" of our relationships including, most of all, total strangers (*RO*:79–100).

On servicing the stranger, Nouwen does place a determined focus. For one, he believes with disarming simplicity that "[t]he call to ministry is the call to be a host to the many strangers passing by."[42] It pays to be reminded that in Romans 12:13, the practice of hospitality involves two movements of caring: "one within the community and one beyond it"[43]—and that certainly includes strangers.

Hospitality, for Nouwen, involves "the creation of a free space where the stranger can enter and become a friend instead of an enemy. Hospitality is not to change people, but to offer them space where change can take place."[44] Indeed, the Bible's command to extend hospitality to strangers (Heb 13:2) urges us to open up an avenue "where strangeness breeds not estrangement, but engagement" instead.[45] The intentional move at welcoming strangers can powerfully translate into a bridge-building act.

Hospitality is love expressed concretely in other-centered fashion. Its paradox lies in "ask[ing] for the creation of an empty space where the guest can find his [*sic*] own soul" (*WH*:92). By the same token, it is not "a subtle invitation to adopt the life style of the host, but the gift of a chance for the guest to find his own" (*RO*:72).

Hospitality itself can be transformed into a healing community—even as it "creates a unity based on the shared confession of our basic brokenness and on our shared hope" (*RO*:93–94). This shows the expansiveness of Nouwen's concept of hospitality. To Nouwen, all of ministry can be reckoned as hospitality.[46] It represents one of the two major acts of compassionate service a Christian can render. The other act, which is bound by the same unified spirit of compassion and solidarity, deals with the challenging realm of social justice—which is our next topic.

Service of Working for Social Justice

Author Ronald Rolheiser considers working for social justice as one of the essential pillars of the spiritual life, a mandatory undertaking consistent with Jesus' teaching that leaves no room for equivocation.[47] We see unmistakably in the New Testament that the way of Jesus is the way of justice. In keeping therefore with what is believed to be at the heart of the biblical expectation for Christian communities, we all need to be actively engaged in working for a just society. It is sad to say, however, that many Christians, along with their respective communities, are missing in action on the battlefield of injustice.

Liberation theologian Gustavo Gutiérrez relentlessly reminds us that if conversion truly results in a radical transformation of ourselves as well as our communities, as many of us claim it does, then it must translate into a whole new way of thinking, feeling, and living—which believes Christ is "present in exploited and alienated persons."[48] As one other Catholic priest so well stated it, "...transformation cannot be a purely interior phenomenon; the energy it generates radiates out and modifies social structures. Thus, the person, changed by conversion, becomes a source of transforming energy for society and the world."[49] In Henri Nouwen's words, "...the change of the human heart and the change of human society are no separable tasks but interconnected as the two beams of the cross."[50]

Theologian Margaret Miles laments over the unfortunate reality that for most Christians, the norm of Christian service has more to do with giving to charity or relieving of immediate need instead of getting actively involved in the critique and reform of societies. As to why many do not see establishing just social arrangements to be an essential part of Christian service, Miles conjectures that many, like Augustine, view injustice as both an inevitable and irreversible result of human fallenness.[51] Consequently, they fail to take appropriate action against the rampant injustices present in our midst.

Henri Nouwen, however, insists that "[a]ction with and for those who suffer is the concrete expression of the compassionate life" (C:120). Jesus Christ himself, in both his teachings and conduct, exemplified compassion that always led to action.[52] In a more specific way, action inevitably entails honest, direct—but humble—confrontation. Nouwen explains in poignant detail why this position is both possible and a necessary expression of real compassion:

> The illusion of power must be unmasked, idolatry must be undone, oppression and exploitation must be...confronted.

We cannot suffer with the poor when we are unwilling to confront those persons and systems that cause poverty. We cannot set the captives free when we do not want to confront those who carry the keys. We cannot profess our solidarity with those who are oppressed when we are unwilling to confront the oppressor. Compassion without confrontation fades quickly into fruitless sentimental commiseration. (C:124)

These are definitely not empty words from someone who does not know what he is talking about. Nouwen's journals, especially *¡Gracias!*, reveal the rock-solid conviction of a man who has been on the battlefront. In his biography of Nouwen, Michael Ford spends no less than a chapter chronicling Nouwen's burning interest in issues of peace and social justice. He tells of how Henri Nouwen

led retreats for Nicaragua's Sandinista leaders, and for U.S. senators and military personnel, and also spoke out against the Gulf War, led worship with protesters at nuclear test sites in Nevada, and visited activists in jail....[H]e also believed in ongoing resistance against the forces of violence, including nonviolent action against militarism and public calls for nuclear disarmament; forming, joining, or living in communities of active nonviolence such as Sojourners, the Catholic Worker, or Pax Christi; and living and working among the poor and broken.[53]

Nouwen modeled concretely how an individual in community can minister and serve the world by working to promote social justice through active engagement with it.

To Nouwen, then, the ministry of spirituality is, at bottom, the ministry of service to Christ for the sake of others employed within the broad setting of community. It is the service of ministry in community, by the community, to the larger community. The umbrella of community soaked in the environment of prayer defines the contour of ministry. Compassionate service in the spirit of solidarity—concretized in both the acts of hospitality and working for social justice—constitutes the praxis of ministry.

Ministry: A Journey Outward

Loving others by reaching out to our fellow human beings is what embodies the real essence of ministry. On this same account hinges the second movement in Henri Nouwen's conceptual framework of the spiritual life. Ministry is about moving toward others. In short, the outward journey is in every way a ministry journey. Henri Nouwen gives us a glimpse, mainly through his writings, of how he himself actively engaged this outward journey as a minister.

Henri Nouwen: The Minister

The ministry journey for Henri Nouwen was naturally broad and all-encompassing. As a minister, he functioned more as a generalist than a specialist, instinctively combining the dynamics of soul care and spiritual formation into a singular thrust—holistically engaging the disciplines of the mind, heart, and body in order to create space for God.[54] Such an integrated mindset and approach account for much of his practical, effective style of ministry—whether it be in his writing, teaching, counseling, spiritual mentoring, guidance, or direction.

Pastor, Priest, Prophet

Indicative of such holistic ministry approach, Nouwen combined the ministerial tasks of *healing*, *sustaining*, and *guiding*, which all stand for the same foundational principles of pastoral theology advocated by Seward Hiltner, one of his mentors at Meninger Clinic. Integrating them into his own applied understanding, Henri Nouwen recast these three shepherding functions into the overlapping roles of a *pastor* (one who heals the wounds of the past), a *priest* (one who sustains life in the present), and a *prophet* (one who guides others to the future) (*LR:75*).

In his ministry of formation, Henri Nouwen wore all three hats, so to speak, in ways that seemed almost indistinguishable. It is difficult if not impossible to pigeonhole Nouwen into one exclusive role, for he assumed a variety of different ones as he ministered to the equally varying needs of people. Depending on the need or situation, Nouwen displayed flexibility in his ministry style and approach. Conversant with a whole gamut of soul care and spiritual formation helps—including spiritual friendship, spiritual guidance, spiritual mentoring, and spiritual direction, Nouwen was able to make productive use of their combined elements with creativity and ease.[55] To use our current lingo, Nouwen was a versatile "multitasker."

Integrated Ministerial Dynamics

Henri Nouwen's ministry of spirituality was inseparable from his spirituality of ministry. The themes of communion, community, and ministry served as intersecting threads weaving his identity as a minister. Ministry is impossible apart from a life of communion with God. Communion yields ministry and ministry creates community.

Any kind of spiritual ministry ought always to be interpreted against the context of spirituality as a social construct. Nouwen believed that a real minister is a convener[56]—a task he equated with the exercise of a form of hospitality. As far as he was concerned, all of ministry is to be seen as hospitality: "To help, to serve, to care, to guide, to heal…[are] all used to express a reaching out toward our neighbor whereby we perceive life as a gift not to possess but to share" (*RO*:109).

This is what soul care is: a selfless sharing of one's life motivated by a deep caring for another person's life. As Nouwen defines it, care "is the loving attention given to another person" (*GG*:58). In essence, "[c]are is compassion" (*BJ*:February 8). And compassion is the sine qua non of soul care. That is why for Nouwen, "the care of the soul is paramount, not the cure of the soul, as a necessary first step in deepening one's own spirituality."[57]

Ministry's Thrust

Given his conviction, Henri Nouwen is unapologetically against what he terms the "professionalization" of ministry whereby various forms of helping and healing become equated with the exercise of power rather than the expression of true service (see *RO*:93, 91). Nouwen is persuaded that "the pastoral relationship can never completely be understood within the logic of a professional contract" (*CM*:57). Ministry ought to be seen more as a mutual alliance between the minister and the one ministered unto.

Mutuality in Ministry

If something needs to be inculcated constantly in the mind of ministers, it is the critical understanding that ministry is "a communal and mutual experience" (*INJ*:40). Service does not have to be a one-way street. We minister as we ourselves are ministered to. We give as needy people who are also willing to receive in the process.

The New Testament is replete with passages that address mutuality in ministry within the context of community life. One cannot possibly ignore the "one another" texts featured in the epistles: admonishing one another (Rom 15:7), encouraging one another (1 Thess 5:11), bearing one another's burdens (Gal 6:2), to name a few.

Formational Ministry

As far as his ultimate aim in ministry, Henri Nouwen was clear-headed about it: "...to lay down [his] life for [his] friends" (*CM*:114). Like Paul, he was only too willing to sacrifice in order for Christ to be fully formed in others (see Gal 4:19). Clearly, for Nouwen, the focal thrust of his ministry was formational. Yet he was under no illusion to claim that it was his job to form others. Henri Nouwen looks at spiritual formation as the process of emptying our heart for the Spirit to be released to do his work.[58] The work of soul care and spiritual formation is really the work of God's Spirit.

Henri Nouwen is wise enough to understand that "the point of spiritual formation is to discern where something is happening...[where] God is doing something. Our task is to become aware of where and how God is presently acting and to recognize that indeed it is God who is acting."[59] We need only to cooperate with him.

In pondering the ministry as a whole, Nouwen leaves us with this vital perspective to integrate into our thinking: "All functions of ministry are life giving. Whether a man [*sic*] teaches, preaches, counsels, plans, or celebrates, his aim is to open new perspectives, to offer new insight, to give new strength, to break through the chains of death and destruction, and to create new life which can be affirmed (*CM*:115)."

Spirituality's Coinherence with Ministry

The earlier discussion on the interface between spirituality and psychology dealt with the knowledge of God and knowledge of self. It is important to qualify that the kind of knowledge we speak of here is not merely intellectual or objective but also existential or experiential knowledge—one that spontaneously merges with the love of God.[60] To know God is to love God since God himself is love. God can only be genuinely known through love—not just objectively as though from a distance, but also subjectively through a close personal encounter.[61]

What is therefore true of the experiential knowledge of God is implicitly true too of the experiential knowledge of the self. In other words, to know and experience the self, in a way, assumes the necessity of loving the self—in a healthy, scripturally warranted way.

Henri Nouwen tells us that if we are to take seriously the Bible's command to love our neighbor as our self, there has to be a good enough love relationship with our true self in place. We cannot give or share of ourselves to others if we do not have a self that we fully accept, intimately know and understand—one that is ultimately worth offering to others. Ministry requires precisely that—the "giving of self" (*G!*:85; cf. *CM*:51). Therefore, to the degree that we love ourselves, we are able to love and give of ourselves to others—but only because we love God in the first place. The Great Commandment in its totality reveals spirituality's coinherence not just with psychology but with ministry as well.

Loving God, Loving Others

Unquestionably for Henri Nouwen, the love of God and the love of neighbor just cannot be separated (cf. 1 John 4:20–21). From the way Nouwen unpacks the dynamic of the Great Commandment, "The first commandment receives concreteness and specificity through the second; the second…becomes possible through the first" (*LR*:32).

Loving God enables us to truly love others; loving others proves that we truly love God. The melding of these two corresponds to the marriage between spirituality and ministry. They cannot be divorced from each other just as the love of God and the love of humanity cannot separately exist and be fulfilled without the other.

From a practical perspective, ministry must be fueled by genuine spirituality for it to be effective; for spirituality to be authentic, it must give birth to actual practice of ministry. Both simply go hand in hand. Spirituality and ministry must therefore be lived out in creative balance. Among other things, this necessitates both willingness and know-how on our part to confront the unavoidable tension between the interiority and exteriority of our lived experience.

Interiority and Exteriority

Writer Owen Thomas charges that in both traditional and contemporary literature about Christian spirituality, "a pervasive emphasis and focus has been on the inner or interior life as distinct from the outer, bodily, and communal life."[62] He asserts that this overemphasis on interiority needs to "be redressed not only to a more balanced view of the inner/outer relation but also to a redirected focus on the outer as primary and as a major source of the inner." Foremost on Thomas's agenda is a vigorous call for a major reformulation of much of the theory and practice of Christian spirituality in order to bring both to a new coherence.[63]

In response to such a call and as a direct challenge to the growing subscription of many to the so-called spirituality of "inwardness" (which some perceive as coming perilously close to withdrawal and disengagement from the world), a good number of Christians rally behind what Margaret Miles calls a more embodied spirituality rooted in Christian practices.[64]

In truth, there is much to commend concerning Thomas's critique on the prevailing excessive focus on interiority. Henri Nouwen, himself, in appreciation for his own exposure to liberation spirituality unashamedly confessed to being guilty of such a skewed focus:

> But as I reflect on the impact of this spirituality on my way of living and thinking, I realize that a reductionism has taken place on my side. I became aware of how individualistic and elitist my own spirituality had been. It was hard to confess, but true, that in many respects my thinking about the spiri-

tual life had been deeply influenced by my North America milieu with its emphasis upon the "interior life" and the methods and techniques for developing that life.[65]

Indeed, it is to our peril if we ignore some of the well-merited warnings Thomas issues out. However, if his major concern, as he claims, is to bring both the theory and practice of spirituality to a fresh coherence, it seems that his agenda would be better served by advocating the necessity of balance and integration instead of reinforcing the already existing polarization between the so-called inner and outer life.

If in fact the whole of the Christian's life is placed under the lordship of Christ, then we would not have to make so sharp a distinction between our inner and outer spirituality, as though they are separate compartments of our Christian life. Kenneth Leech thinks that the erroneous assumption that spirituality is just about the "inner life"—which is largely responsible for the widespread split between *spirituality* and *social justice*—lies in the equally distorted concept of spirituality as merely a "dimension" rather than the whole of life.[66]

Even in the history of theology, the "delicate balance between the spiritual and moral spheres of life has not always been maintained with care...."[67] But, as ethicist Dennis Hollinger correctly insists, spirituality and ethics ought not to be far apart from each other since "the moral life...must always be tied to the internal dimension of Christian experience, and the internal dimension must always demonstrate itself in the external dimension, including both word and deed."[68]

This dualistic sway in traditional moral theology has been severely criticized by different proponents of political and liberation theology who, Owen Thomas claims, have continually harped on "the centrality of the outer actions of seeking justice."[69] However, contrary to what is commonly believed, the real focus of liberation theology goes far deeper than action and ethics into its mystical foundation.[70]

Whether or not we are willing to accept fully what liberation theologians stand for, their brand of spirituality does represent a genuine attempt to critically balance the tension between interiority and exteriority. For instance, the Chilean writer Segundo

Galilea, has consistently stressed the concept of integral liberation in which social engagement and interior transformation go hand in hand.[71] For him, "contemplation is a quality of action and action a quality of contemplation."[72]

Henri Nouwen approvingly regards contemplation and ministry as going hand in hand. Ministry is seen as a necessary extension of a contemplative life (CM:63). He expounds on the vital link between contemplation and ministry in this way: "To contemplate is to *see* and to minister is to make visible. The contemplative life is a life with a vision and the life of a ministry is the life in which this vision is revealed to others."[73]

Despite more recent efforts by liberation theologians to realign and balance our thinking about interiority and exteriority in our spiritual life, it would be consciously naïve on our part to ignore the lingering impression of many that the practice of spirituality throughout history has been fraught with a heavy focus on the inner world at the expense of the outer world of active social participation (which Owen Thomas already described earlier in pinpoint detail). While such allegations have been proven true to a certain extent, they do not represent a complete historical picture and assessment of the actual situation. Philip Sheldrake helps adjust the popular yet misguided thinking of many on this matter.

To cite an example, a thorough study of ancient monasticism shows that the temporary practice of withdrawal from a sin-ridden location to a place of solitude and cleansing such as the desert was never originally meant to be an escapist route for people to establish an alternative society. Sheldrake shows through the documented lives of the monastics like Antony and Simeon Stylites that they did not entirely leave their social or public roles behind. He notes, "...by standing (geographically and socially) outside normal boundaries, the ascetic was accepted as a spiritual guide and social arbitrator."[74] In a way, monasticism assumed a prophetic role, a subversive act of resistance at the heart of all systems while suggesting alternate visions of what human community could be.[75]

The same can be said of the true practice of Western mysticism, which has often been construed by many as inherently inward, when in reality it carried with it profound social and ethical implications. Even contemporary writer Evelyn Underhill, whose book *Mysticism* stands as one of the modern classics of the last century, viewed Christian mysticism as that union with the divine that "impels a person towards an active, outside, rather than purely passive, inward life."[76]

Henri Nouwen himself concluded, after reading Underhill's *The Mystics of the Church*, that "[i]t is one of the most convincing arguments for the Christian belief that the love of God lived in its fullest sense leads to a most selfless dedication to the neighbor." Mysticism, Nouwen came to be convinced, does not imply withdrawal from the world; for it is precisely our "[i]ntimate union with God [that] leads to the most creative involvement in the contemporary world" (*GD*:177).

In summary, Christian spirituality, as Philip Sheldrake concludes, involves the "dialectic of the mystical and prophetic." The concepts of interiority and exteriority therefore express "complementary dimensions" that must always be held in creative tension.[77] Such tension is to be expected if one is to seriously balance the coinherent reality of spirituality and ministry in one's experience.

Conclusion

A thoughtful exploration of the intersection between spirituality and ministry—one that takes into account the inherent tension between the interiority and exteriority of our lived experience—facilitates a more integrated view of our spiritual life and its formation. Against the beleaguered distinctions we make between the inward and the outward dynamics of the spiritual life—which only betrays our reductive propensity to constitute such terms as binary opposites—we need to realize that these needlessly imposed distinctions do not have to be so polarized as to be of little or no conceptual value.

Exploration of the spiritual dynamics between our interiority and exteriority creates renewed recognition of how various concepts such as loving God, loving others, communion and community, prayer and service, contemplation and action, mystical and prophetic are so linked together. Therefore, they can be construed as coinherent and conjoined realities without blinking away their distinct meaning.

Henri Nouwen understood and lived out the significance of this perspective. His shining example proves how the whole issue of balance, though admittedly elusive, is not a totally impossible pursuit as we seek to live out our spirituality—both individually and communally.

CHAPTER THREE

Journey Upward

Focus on Theology and Spirituality

We have uncovered, thus far, how spirituality interweaves with ministry just as psychology does with spirituality. This chapter directs the spotlight on *theology*—which, at base, deals with our upward movement toward God. Theology is the third and final domain that clinches the coinherence trilogy of spirituality. Like psychology and ministry, theology indivisibly fuses with spirituality.

Henri Nouwen believed this to be the case. Conceptually, he saw no discrepancy between the nature of theology and spirituality. At the same time he worked vigorously to maintain their practical integrity in his own day-to-day experience. Nouwen had every reason to do so. The checkered history of the church bears witness to Christianity's struggle time and again to sustain the unity between theology and spirituality. Today, as in the past, their wedded status continues to be imperiled by a constant threat of divorce.

The Great Divide

As spirituality approaches center stage in the life of the Christian community, theology as a discipline seems determined to resist being relegated to the sidelines. Systematic theologians in particular openly frown at the more contemporary expressions of spirituality, which they charge as being heavily identified with any and every kind of conceivable experience.[1] On the other side, advocates of spirituality express nervousness about the resurgent spirituality phenomena being subjected to rigid scrutiny by theologians who are only too eager to systematize anything that they judge to be out of control. Consequently, both camps often tend to take on a defensive stance.

As is in the case of psychology and spirituality, a mutual mistrust plagues the proponents of both theology and spirituality. Worse yet, a sharp divide continues to be erected between the so-called theological profession and spiritual expression of our Christian faith—needlessly dichotomizing doctrine from experience, belief from practice.

Doctrine versus Experience

Given the contemporary ease with which "theology" is commonly referred to as "the body of Christian beliefs,"[2] it is not surprising that "doctrine" becomes automatically aligned with it. Doctrine then gets equated with dogma which, for many, is nothing but a set of cold tenets unrelated to life. Too often doctrine is pitted against experience as if they have no connection with each other.

Summing up the convictions that propel Ellen Charry's groundbreaking work *By the Renewing of Your Minds*, George Lindbeck, in his foreword to Charry's book, states succinctly: "Doctrine is pastoral, theology and spirituality belong together."[3] Still, one would be hard-pressed to counter the all-too-narrow perception of many that doctrine is but the theoretical framework of Christian belief apart from practice, giving the wrong impression that the notion of "practicing Christian doctrine is an oxymoron."[4] As we are about to see, it is this exact presenting problem that Henri Nouwen sought to address in his formation work.

Embodied Truth

Biblically speaking, dimensions of the doctrinal are not at all separate from the practical. The reality of the incarnation of God in Jesus—the Word made flesh—speaks patently of the embodiment of truth. Christian truth—often linked with theology and doctrine—is no more propositional than experiential by virtue of its *enfleshed* character. It cannot today, any more than in the time of the Bible, pass for mere idea, concept, or doctrine in that it incorporates the components of both the objective and subjective.

Truth, as such, is meant not only to be known but, more importantly, to be experienced.

Relational Truth

To truly know something, as educator Parker Palmer unravels, "is to have a living relationship with it—influencing and being influenced by the object known." Truth is after us as much as we are after truth, Parker is quick to remind us.[5] Truth may, then, be said to inhabit the realm of the relational as well as the communal as it always lodges itself within the context of a live relationship. As John's Gospel attests, the essence of spiritual life entails the knowledge of truth within the context of an interactive, communal relationship (see John 17:3).

Henri Nouwen clarified that when Jesus sent the Holy Spirit, it was so "we may be led to the full truth of the divine life."[6] Jesus claims to be *the* Truth himself (see John 14:6). Truth, therefore, ought to be seen in terms of a real, intimate relationship with the living Christ.

Linking truth with the notion of intimacy implies that as an intimate reality itself, it is as much a matter of the intellect as it is of the heart. In connecting it with the true knowledge of God, John Calvin painstakingly distinguished truth from "that knowledge which, content with empty speculation, merely fits in the brain," to "that which will be sound and fruitful if we duly perceive it, and it takes root in the heart."[7] Theologian William Placher distills Calvin's thinking this way: "Apprehension of God is thus, as in Aquinas, wisdom, *sapientia*, rather than knowledge, *scientia*—that is, practical rather than speculative."[8] Such a classic notion, in our day, has unfortunately fallen on hard times. To recover this lost concept of *sapiential* theology, according to Ellen Charry, would require reviving the pastoral function of theology where doctrine becomes normative again instead of simply descriptive—employing "the wisdom of God that makes for an excellent life."[9]

Outworking of Truth

One intriguing side note is that the classic spiritual texts of the past are generally not fixated around doctrinal concepts and speculations as much as the actual living of the Christian life. Philip

Sheldrake reminds us that the true rationale behind doctrinal clarification "is always to express, promote and protect a quite distinctive experience of God along with its practical implications for life and prayer."[10] It is not that the ancient texts do not address doctrines or deal with theological constructs at all, but the main focus of the writings usually has more to do with the practical outworking of the Christian truths in real experience.

The famous *Showings* (often called *Revelations of Divine Love*) by Julian of Norwich is a sterling example of a classic work that is doctrinally based yet practical enough for pastoral teaching. Julian concerned herself more with "a knowledge that arises from participation and love rather than something that depends on purely rational inquiry."[11] This does not mean that Julian did not do real theology at all. She did superb theology and went even beyond that; she lived out her theology fully. It is fair to say that Julian's dialectic approach to theology well represented English piety during her era, which typified "harmony and balance between the affective and the speculative."[12]

The same theological and experiential dynamics in Julian were present in Teresa of Ávila's works. Most evident was the continual interplay between experience and doctrine wherein "[t]he weft of her theoretical and practical teaching [was] skillfully carried through the warp of her concrete experience."[13] This was the case too for Ignatius of Loyola and St. John of the Cross. Both of them connected spirituality and theology by basing their scriptural and theological reflections respectively upon their own concrete spiritual experiences.[14] All these examples validate J. Matthew Ashley's insightful observation that "daring articulations of the experience of God arising from within the history of Christian spirituality can breathe new life into theological systems that have become too closed in on themselves and too obsessed with the drive to logical consistency."[15]

Nouwen's Example

Henri Nouwen's own spiritual example is a modern version of this creative phenomenon at work. Nouwen insisted on the imperative to "situate our knowledge of God in the concrete circumstances of our existence."[16] To him, our doctrinal life is never to be disengaged from our life of faith. Doctrine and experience seemed to merge almost seamlessly in Nouwen's way of life.

One easily gathers this impression by dipping into the pages of *Letters to Marc*, a compelling and sound doctrinal formulation of Nouwen's uncompromising theological position about the person of Jesus. Nouwen made it explicit from the very start—despite the obvious theological tenor of his letters—that he was not writing in abstract terms; he was rather conveying what he himself has "lived out and lived through." Everything revolved around Nouwen's personal relationship with Jesus, which was at the heart of his existence. "Living with Jesus at the center" defined for Henri Nouwen what it meant to live spiritually (*LM*:6–7).

Letters to Marc broadly captures Nouwen's doctrine of the spiritual life—one in which the experience of his own faith was enfleshed. Henri Nouwen by no means exhibited perfect balance in his spiritual life, but his writings show that he genuinely strove for consistency and integrity in living out his spirituality.[17]

Belief versus Practice

Closely identified with the existing bifurcation of doctrine and experience is the breach between belief and practice. Herein lies the tension many wrestle with on an ongoing basis. There lurks a resigned sense that one's theological beliefs do not seem to matter much nowadays. Many people regard them as irrelevant or marginally significant due to what most witness to be doctrine's woeful detachment from the everyday life of faith. The ever-widening split between faith and practice is almost becoming a normative reality for many.

Existence of a Gap

It is sobering to realize that we all experience a gap between what we say we believe and how we live out our belief. Our *orthodoxy* (right belief or thinking) does not often connect with our *orthopathy* (right attitude or affect) and our *orthopraxy* (right practice or action).

If anybody has transparently demonstrated before the watching world the persistence of such a gap, Henri Nouwen did. Jean Vanier made this remark about Nouwen: "Henri lived out the contradictions that all of us experience, between Gospel values and worldly values, between what we say and what we actually live. That was his poverty. It is the poverty of us all."[18]

Similarly, if ever there was someone who showed intense commitment to bridging that same gap, it was Henri Nouwen. True saintliness for Nouwen meant "living without division between word and action." He sincerely wanted to pattern his own life after the example of Jesus, who truly was "the Word made flesh"—the one in whom "no division existed between his words and his actions, between what he said and what he did."[19]

Theological Reflection: Bridging the Gap

Following Thomas Merton, Henri Nouwen adopted the style of personal narration to reflect critically on himself and to mesh his thought and action. Through this process called theological reflection, one's personal experience is examined from a decidedly Christian grid for the express purpose of transformation on both the individual and corporate levels. Catholic theologian James Bacik deftly describes Merton's autobiographical style of theological pondering as reflective of "rigorous honesty and [an] amazing capacity for self-criticism" even as he tried to explore and connect the Christian tradition to real-life issues, thus inspiring many to be more effective interpreters of their own stories.[20] The same vivid descriptions can appropriately be applied also to Henri Nouwen.

Both Merton and Nouwen utilized their written journals as an effective tool for personal theological reflection. As an avid memoirist and diarist, Henri Nouwen seems, in my opinion, to surpass Merton. I agree with Robert Waldron: "Nouwen's genius was his own transparency. Merton aimed for transparency and sometimes achieved it. Nouwen didn't have to try: it was very much a part of his personality."[21]

It should not therefore come as a surprise that Henri Nouwen would be a natural and an eager advocate of the discipline of personal reflection. In his book *Can You Drink the Cup?*, Nouwen prompts us all to keep cultivating this critical practice:

[J]ust living a life is not enough. We must know what we are living. A life that is not reflected upon isn't worth living. It belongs to the essence of being human that we contemplate our life, think about it, discuss it, evaluate it, and form opinions about it. Half of living is reflecting on what is being lived. Reflection is essential for growth, development, and change. It is the unique power of the human person.[22]

Theological reflection became a useful tool for Nouwen to consciously bridge the gap between his *professed* and *expressed* theology—between what he believed and how he actually functioned in life. In fact Nouwen's decision to move to L'Arche was said to be driven by a desire to close the gap between what he wrote and what he lived.[23]

Combining Faith and Practice

In a positive sense, people who employ the art and discipline of theological reflection on a consistent basis are constrained to combine faith and practice more tightly. Those of us who are acutely aware of the perennial gap existing between our beliefs and practices need also to realize that while beliefs shape our practices, practices can and do affect our beliefs as well.

Lived spirituality is really about "attending with as much authenticity as one can muster to the truth of one's own experience"[24] "An authentic life," Eugene Peterson describes, "is one in which there is congruence between the truths asserted and the life lived."[25] Theological probity must go hand in hand with spiritual vitality if we are to be serious about lending substance to our faith more authentically. Belief and practice, like doctrine and experience, need to be intentionally merged because they belong together just as theology and spirituality are connected tightly together.

Ironically, the now discredited Enlightenment paradigm—with the debunking of the "myth of objectivity" in the West—is gradually paving the way for the reconnection of the original link between theology and spirituality.[26] For one, constructive postmodernism subscribes to more holistic and integrative approaches to understanding that allow for mystery and tension and promote mutuality and relationship in wholeness.[27] As such, theology and spirituality—properly defined and understood—can and must be rewoven within the frame of our postmodern time.

True Essence of Theology and Spirituality

Before getting to the heart of the relationship between spirituality and theology, we should formally establish their basic definitions within a decidedly Christian context. Any attempt to correlate them ultimately hinges upon our agreed understanding of their core meanings.

Nature of Theology

The weighty term *Christian theology* is generally taken to mean "a set of ideas which are recognizably grounded in the Christian tradition, having its origins in the Bible and maintained and developed in the process of reflection, interpretation and transmission within the community of faith."[28] From this widely accepted definition, it is understandable why most people easily characterize theology as the *theory* while spirituality is the *practice* of the Christian life—an attempt that is simplistic at best, potentially misleading at worst.

The implication behind this popular view is that while the two may be somewhat connected, spirituality and theology remain as independent entities and, therefore, are not duly integrated into each other. Such narrow thinking is the result of a myopic understanding of theology.

In its classic sense, theology is historically understood as "a heartfelt knowledge of divine things," according to Edward Farley, with the coinherence of intellect and piety in clear view.[29] Based on this holistic understanding, the faculties of the mind and the heart are intimately engaged. Many of us live in a time when people's ideas about theology are nowhere close to the original vision that Farley articulated so intently.

Theology as Prayer

Henri Nouwen notes that "the first time the word *theologia* was used within the Christian tradition, it referred to the highest level of prayer" and that the desert fathers and mothers identified it in terms associated with "a direct intimate communion with God."[30] Evagrius of Pontus himself once remarked: "To be a theologian is to pray truly and to pray truly is to be a theologian."[31] Henri Nouwen elucidates this notion further:

> True theology creates the inner space in which God's word can happen to us. The purpose of theological understanding is not to grasp, control, or even use God's word, but to become increasingly willing to let the word of God speak to us, guide us, move us, and lead us to places far beyond our own comprehension. Thus theology *is* prayer.[32]

"[M]uch theology," Nouwen accedes, "asked questions 'from below,' shedding light only in one realm of reality. Real theology...could access answers 'from above,' of the higher, deeper eternal realm."[33]

Transformational and Creative

Theology, if it is real, is supposed to change people. In the first place, "[a]ll true theology is about transformation...through the encounter with the true God."[34] Change begins with the mind. Deep theological thinking that brings about change and renewal is, for Henri Nouwen, a way of thinking that fully employs the mind of Christ.[35] At the same time, the mind engages the heart deeply and creatively—in a sort of mystical fashion.

Transformation is nonlinear; it is never a systematized event but a creative process. With this mentality and conviction, Henri Nouwen flatly refused to reckon theology as a system; for him, it is more of an artistry.[36] Far from being a fossilized reality, authentic theology is one that breathes life, creative life.

Philip Sheldrake stands convinced that "[a] theology that is alive is always grounded in spiritual experience."[37] In the final analysis, theology is foremost a spiritual enterprise. Implicit here is theology's natural tie-in with spirituality. The very essence of theology does commingle with the true nature of spirituality.

The Nature of Spirituality

In wading through the vast resources on the subject of spirituality and wringing from it every bit of description it provides, we are still challenged to settle on a rudimentary definition of its nature. A general survey of Christian spirituality contained in both old and current literature only yields elaborate features that belie an easily integrated summarization.[38] Little wonder that one author wryly labeled spirituality as a term vague enough, in current diction, to be a "catch-all" that catches nothing definite.[39]

Life in the Spirit

Nevertheless, spirituality, especially Christian spirituality—even though lacking in definitional precision—has to have some conceptual limits for it to mean something of real substance, Philip Sheldrake insists. He supplies us with the most succinct working definition of Christian spirituality: "life in the Spirit."[40]

The distinct focus is on the lived experience of our spiritual life. Sheldrake's description serves as an apt distillation of Henri Nouwen's collective grasp of the true essence of the spiritual life—which is the experiential way we live out our life in Christ through the enabling power of the Holy Spirit. Simple as it may sound, Nouwen's conception of Christian spirituality is actually comprehensive in nature. His treatment of the subject in several of his writings surfaces its far-reaching implications.

Spirituality According to Nouwen

First of all, Henri Nouwen recognizes that our spiritual life is a gift, a supernatural one at that, since the life we now live, spiritually speaking, is strictly not our own; it is "life lived in the spirit of Jesus" (*MN*:65). Paul the apostle speaks of this reality when he claims, "...it is no longer I who live, but it is Christ who lives in me" (Gal 2:20). Furthermore, this spiritual life refers to a new quality of life because it represents "the life of those reborn from above—who have received the Spirit of God who comes to us from God" (*HN*:55).

Henri Nouwen's idea of spirituality is grounded in the reality of the present. He insists that "the spiritual life is not a life before, after, or beyond our everyday existence. [It] can only be real when it is lived in the midst of the pains and joys of the here and now." (*MN*:21) To Nouwen, our life in the Spirit represents our continuing response to the invitation of Jesus for us to enter and embrace an intimate, fruitful, and ecstatic life, born and nurtured not within the context of fear but of love (see *LS*).

Henri Nouwen calls us to celebrate the wonder of the spiritual life with the ringing affirmation of being loved by God, convinced that this truth represents the very essence of our existence. He vigorously insists on our holding to our true identity as the beloved children of God, for ultimately it is what provides substance to our life in the Spirit. He does not, however, simply bask in this precious truth; he wants it to be incarnated in our journey as we move intentionally from *being* to *becoming* God's beloved on an experiential level. This journeying process is all-embracing: "*Becoming the Beloved means letting the truth of our Belovedness become enfleshed in everything we think, say or do.*" In emphasizing this aspect, Henri Nouwen ushers us to the important realization that claiming and affirming our true spiritual nature is but the beginning of the spiritual life. Without apology, he lets us come face to face with the full life of the beloved: "chosen and blessed" yet "broken and given" for the sake of others (*LOB*:28, 103, 37, 39).

Indeed, "those who have entered into the spiritual life," Nouwen indicated, "are precisely the ones who are sent into the world to continue and fulfill the work that Jesus began" (*MN*:45). Nouwen's remark stresses the truth that our full life with God is a spiritual confluence of inward realities and outward expressions. Christian spirituality is about God's life freely flowing from us to others.

While our spirituality is a gift, living it out requires our active participation and cooperation with God. Henri Nouwen spells out that real struggle is required to "allow God's Spirit to work in us and recreate us" (*MN*:65, 94). Spirituality is foremost about change and constant renewal of life. The entirety of the spiritual journey involves the ongoing process of conversion and transformation.

Ultimately, the nature of spirituality for Henri Nouwen is integrative. It encompasses the unified movement to our innermost self, to our fellow human beings and to our God—tying in with the love of self, neighbor, and God—which is the threefold focus of the Great Commandment. Here we can detect not only the intertwining relationship of spirituality with psychology and ministry, but also the dynamic interplay between theology and spirituality.

Interplay between Theology and Spirituality

It bears pointing out that the alleged tension between theology and spirituality is not essentially between *theology* and spirituality per se, but, as theologian Alister McGrath rightly delineates it, "...between *modern western concepts of theology and spirituality*," which are more rational than relational.[41]

Many advocates of spirituality tend to react to such highly abstract constructions of theology. Perhaps this is why scholars like Bernard McGinn choose to subscribe to the primacy of spirituality, refusing to subordinate it to the sole scrutiny of dogmatic theology.[42]

In part, such constructions may also explain some people's misgivings in embracing the interdependency between theology and spirituality. Sandra Schneiders, for one, firmly holds that while the two may function as close partners in the conversation, theology and spirituality need to retain their independence from each other.[43]

Philip Sheldrake suggests a *via media* in which we construe the relationship between theology and spirituality as distinct yet not exactly autonomous as they are actually evaluative of each other. Their relationship has more of a reciprocal dynamic.

In this case, Sheldrake's proposal makes sense as it places equal weight on the interdependent roles the two disciplines play. Instead of dichotomy, their dialectical nature calls for reintegration. In examining more closely their reciprocity, it is vital to keep in mind that "...spirituality without theology runs the danger of becoming private or interior. Theology, however, needs the corrective of spirituality to remind us that true knowledge of God concerns the heart as much as the intellect."[44] Balance, as always, is in order.

In reality, as Mark McIntosh submits, both spirituality and theology stand on a common ground, which is "encounter with God."[45] Strictly speaking, one commences such an encounter with the explicit base of theology as its starting point. It is, however, a theology characterized by a *Godward* encounter, an upward journey whose process is spiritual through and through.

Theology: A Movement toward God

The moment we speak of God, we invoke the language of theology. Theology is, first and foremost, about God. Yet it is, as we already know, more than just about God—it involves encountering God. Every encounter entails movement—ours and God's.

Henri Nouwen intimates a sense of the mysterious dynamic involved in such an encounter between the human and the divine by stating that "God should be sought, but we cannot find God. We can only be found by him" (*GD*:116). How exactly this happens, it is hard to know for certain. One can only conjecture since no one can possibly fathom God's ways and divine initiatives.

From a human standpoint though, one encounters God by journeying toward him. Metaphorically speaking, this upward (or Godward) journey symbolizes one's effort to reach out—or better yet, reach up—to God. In Henri Nouwen's paradigmatic scheme, this journey rounds off the threefold movement of the spiritual life.

Reaching Up to God in Prayer

How does one go about reaching up to God? God's preferred way seems to be via the mystery of prayer. Henri Nouwen believes that "by directing ourselves totally to…God,…prayer lifts us up into the timeless immortal life of God" (*RP*:21). It fuels our journey toward him. Nouwen elaborates: "In prayer I can enter into contact with the God who created me and all things out of love. In prayer I can find a new sense of belonging since it is there that I am most related" (*GD*:130). Thus he concludes, "Prayer is the most concrete way to make our home in God" (*LS*:39).

Despite his solid convictions about prayer, Nouwen still struggled with his own prayer life. One of his last entries in his diary contains this revealing confession: "After sixty-three years of life and thirty-eight years of priesthood, my prayer seems as dead as a rock" (*SJ*:5). While reflecting more deeply on the pathetic state of his personal prayer life, Nouwen tried questioning himself:

Are the darkness and dryness of my prayer signs of God's absence or are they signs of a presence deeper and wider than my senses can contain? Is the death of my prayer the death of my intimacy with God or the beginning of a new communion, beyond words, emotions, and bodily sensations?

(*SJ*:6)

Whatever his answers might have been to his own questions, one thing stands out: Nouwen's comprehension of prayer points beyond the level of conversation to the highest and most profound level of communion with God.

Communion As Union with God in Prayer

As Henri Nouwen reminds us, the overwhelming desire of the human heart is communion—which means "union with." Such union comes to fruition within the rich atmosphere of prayer. Incidentally, Nouwen points out that the original meaning of the word *theology* is "union with God in prayer."[46]

Prayer invites us "to live in ever closer communion with the one who loves us more than any human being can."[47] The experience of praying itself becomes a heart-to-heart matter "where the heart of God is united with the heart that prays. Thus knowing God becomes loving God, just as being known by God is being loved by God" (*BBL*:22–23). Prayer, as Nouwen imagined it, is like God "breathing in us, by which we become part of the intimacy of God's inner life" (*RO*:125).

To conclude this section, let me reemphasize what we have already alluded to earlier: Our journey toward full union with God in glory, while at base theological in its Godward focus, cannot be solely conceived as such. At the level of deep encounter with God, the foundation and process of the journey are both theological and spiritual in essence. Far from being separate entities, theology and spirituality do coinhere together.

Theology's Coinherence with Spirituality

One of the first theology textbooks used by the Harvard University students when it was founded as a training college for ministers in 1636 was *The Marrow of Theology* by the Puritan divine William Ames. In that book, we discover one of the finest definitions of theology ever stated: "Theology is the knowledge of living in the presence of God." This simple but profound definition divulges something of the inner quality of theology as a form of spirituality itself.[48]

Knowing God, Experiencing God

The integration of theology with spirituality makes even greater sense when one recognizes the reality that the knowledge of God and the experience of God, if indeed authentic, are bound to naturally coalesce. In examining the related functioning of heart and mind, Bruce Demarest clarifies that *"the heart discovers and experiences God; reason demonstrates and explains God."* Pressed therefore to its logical relationship, "right-thinking must be wedded to personal experience of God in the core of one's being."[49] Theology and spirituality do interpenetrate so that they form one whole.

This view was prevalent in the first millennium of the Christian era, as James Bacik recounts for us. Back then, "spirituality and theology remained closely united. Theory and practice were not separate categories, but were united in the common goal of following Christ."[50] Theology and spirituality during the patristic period embodied solid unity. This is validated by no less than the patristic scholar Andrew Louth.[51] Sad to say, such unified status of theology and spirituality has not been sustained throughout the fractious history of the church.

Bacik warns of the consequences of theology and spirituality becoming estranged from each other. By speaking a language that barely resonates with the average person in the pew, theology can easily become disconnected from daily existence and the real-life concerns that ordinary people wrestle with. On the other hand, spirituality, without solid theological foundations, runs the risk of becoming "faddish, superficial and unbalanced."[52] In order to maintain their integrity, we must embrace a transformed understanding of theology and spirituality that is at once practical and experiential.

Practical Spirituality, Experiential Theology

The great theologians and spiritual masters of the church prior to the eighteenth century, such as Athanasius, Augustine, Anselm, Aquinas, and Luther, saw no tension "between the intellectual exploration of the faith and its practical outworking in spirituality."[53] Christianity was, for them, as it should be for us, a "practiced theology" and a "lived spirituality."[54]

Once again, Henri Nouwen stands out as a modern example to the contemporary church of one who can provide us a dynamic framework for integrating theology and spirituality. His "popular" brand of theology and spirituality reflects a *story* or a *narrative* quality to it that is orientated to everyday life situations with which lay folks can identify. Richard Mouw illuminates Nouwen's practical approach:

> It is a theological reflection on questions of middle range, a theology aimed at practical wisdom. We are not to help people merely to *cope* with life's quandaries and agonies. We are to *address* those complexities and pains, showing how God's saving work relates to the "seemingly random events" of our lives, so that Christian people can discern "the mind of Jesus" and thereby experience "God's gentle guidance."[55]

All theology is practical, as far as Henri Nouwen is concerned. It is rooted in the actual experiences of actual people caught up in actual situations. Like Anton Boisen, who was one of his heroes, he thought that "the most forgotten source of theology was 'the living human document.'" Nouwen felt the need for an empirical theology whose substance is drawn from the mundane realities we experience everyday (CM:62).

Henri Nouwen demonstrated a commitment to a practical theology of spirituality. In fact, his book *Creative Ministry* was "an impassioned plea to make the practical areas of theology more spiritual."[56] Not only did his commitment mirror itself in his writings but more so in the way he lived out his life. Nouwen became known for "his ability and desire to meet people at their own level, to communicate theological truths in terms ordinary people could understand."[57] James Dittes, chairman of the search committee that offered Nouwen his professorship at Yale, said this about

Nouwen: "He was a pastoral theologian, somebody who made theology existential enough to become a living theology."[58]

Theology was itself a spiritual experience for Nouwen. Reminiscing about his invaluable experience with Adam, the handicapped member of L'Arche Community he was privileged to assist, Nouwen confessed: "After many years of studying, reflecting, and teaching theology, Adam came into my life, and by his life and his heart he announced to me and summarized all I had ever learned."[59]

Above all, Henri Nouwen embraced theological moments as "moments of doxology in which knowing God, loving God, and praising God"[60] are one even as theology and spirituality are one. Inextricably, they are bound together.

Conclusion

Henri Nouwen has forged—however imperfectly—the path for us to follow insofar as maintaining the integrity of theology and spirituality in the context of our times. The guidance he provides can motivate us to keep pursuing a lifestyle of integrity in our own journey.

Integrity is what the Love Commandment is about: loving God with our mind, heart, and strength—bringing together the aspects of our *knowing* (orthodoxy), our *being* (orthopathy), and our *doing* (orthopraxy) in an integrated fashion. Like an unbreakable chain, integrity speaks of the connectedness of *head* (belief), *heart* (feeling), and *hand* (action).

The Great Commandment, in Henri Nouwen's integrated thinking, "is a call to the most profound unity, in which God, God's people, and we ourselves are part of one love." He shows how this unity can be perceived in three interlocking ways:

> First, when we direct our whole beings toward God, we will find our neighbor and ourselves right in the heart of God. Second, when we truly love ourselves as God's beloved children, we will find ourselves in complete unity with our neighbor and with God. Third, when we truly love our neighbor as our brother and sister, we will find, right there, God and ourselves in complete unity. There really is no first, second, and third in the great commandment. All is one: the

heart of God, the hearts of all people, our own hearts. All the great mystics have "seen" this and lived it. (*SJ*:179–80)

To recapitulate: The first three chapters dealt with Henri Nouwen's trilogy of coinherence: spirituality and psychology (knowing *self*, knowing *God*); spirituality and ministry (loving *God*, loving *others*); and spirituality and theology (*knowing* God, *experiencing* God). This trilogy not only corresponds with the threefold focus of the Great Commandment but also draws out at the same time the specific nexus of spirituality with psychology (love of self), with ministry (love of others), and with theology (love of God). In turn, they all coincide with Henri Nouwen's three integrated movements of the spiritual life: to self, others, and God. In conjunction with this particular schema of the spiritual life set forth by Henri Nouwen, author Annice Callahan shows the dynamic of Nouwen's spirituality of the heart arising from "the triple movement into solitude, service, and prayer...qualities of being, attitudes of heart at the level of relationship with ourselves, others, and God."[61]

As a fitting finale, there is yet another integrative way of seeing this threefold dynamic of solitude, service, and prayer unfold through the experience of "real presence" via the creation of free space for ourselves, for others, and for God. It is fused with the inward, outward, and upward dynamics of the spiritual life.

In solitude, we become present to ourselves by creating a free space in our heart to understand who we are; in service, we become present to others by creating a free space for others to understand who they are; in prayer, we become present to God by creating a free space for God to understand who he is.[62] Each of these intersecting spiritual movements serves to highlight the inward, outward, and Godward flow of our journey with God.

PART II

The Imperfect *Journey*

"The imperfect is our paradise."
(Wallace Stevens, "Poems of Our Climate")

"I am unable to say that I have arrived;
I never will in this life...."
(Henri Nouwen, *The Return of the Prodigal Son*)

"Not that I have already obtained all this, or have already been
made perfect, but I press on...."
(Phil 3:12 NIV)

CHAPTER FOUR

Spirituality of Imperfection

Integration and Imperfection

In the life and work of Henri Nouwen, we have witnessed the conceptual and the methodological dynamics of integration exemplified via his coinherent view of the relationships of spirituality, psychology, ministry, and theology. We have also caught a glimpse of how his integrative framework realized itself in his actual ministry of soul care and spiritual formation.

Henri Nouwen's proclivity for integration represented a major step toward wholeness. On a much deeper analysis, his commitment to pursuing integrity spoke more about his heightened awareness of his fractured human condition than an obsessive drive for perfection. Nouwen's integrative pursuit of the spiritual life never obviated but instead incorporated facets of psychological, ministerial, and theological imperfections. For Nouwen, integration coexisted with the glaring realities of imperfection—a phenomenon we are about to examine more closely.

A Psychology of Imperfection

Whatever else may be said about it, integration concerns wholeness. Wholeness, which is more often conceived of in psychological terms to refer to functional well-being, implies a sense of completeness. If viewed narrowly and taken to an extreme, the concept of wholeness can be problematic. The drive toward psychological progress and development, including health, recovery, and healing—while legitimate—can easily be misdirected.

No one can deny our fallenness as human beings. Because of sin, our organic functioning has been impaired. Psychologically and physiologically, we have all been subjected to corruption. Yet it is true that we are capable of experiencing mental and psychological progress and development despite our damaged condition. Substantial healing can take place in our current state. While there is nothing wrong, in and of itself, with seeking health and healing for others and ourselves during this present life, complete wholeness of body, soul, and spirit remains an eschatological reality.[1] The care and cure of souls, Ray Anderson explains, is not about normalizing of pain, distortion, and suffering but their submission to "the reality of an actual healing which is taking place provisionally and will most certainly take place finally."[2]

Wholeness through Brokenness

If, indeed, the interior journey is a prime focus of psychology, then Henri Nouwen effectively put not only the soul, but more importantly, the heart back into psychology. Notwithstanding, it remains an imperfect journey because it involves a soul, a self, a heart that is broken.

Referring to our universal human condition, Henri Nouwen openly admitted: "Our brokenness is so visible and tangible, so concrete and specific" (*LOB*:69). He, of course, spoke as a deeply broken man himself: "...broken with psychological wounds, physical limitations, and emotional needs."[3] Yet with author Frederick Buechner, he subscribed to brokenness as "a way of being human in this world, which is the way to wholeness."[4]

Wholeness is what each of us is after because it is "the way things ought to be." It is what the Hebrews called *shalom*—a term commonly translated "peace," although in the Bible it incorporates the notions of *"universal flourishing, wholeness, and delight."*[5] Drawing from raw episodes in his life, Henri Nouwen testified about experiencing this *shalom*, a wholeness and peace "found in our weakness, in those places of our hearts where we feel most broken, most insecure, most in agony, most afraid."[6]

In one of his diaries, Nouwen expressed with gut-wrenching honesty his convoluted feelings of abandonment, restlessness, anxiety, and loneliness that all seemed determined to haunt him forever. Despite the constant bleeding that his inner wound continued to inflict upon him, Nouwen reckoned it not only as "a gift in disguise," but also as "a gateway to [his] salvation, a door to glory, and a passage to freedom!" (*SJ*:24–25)

Blessing of Brokenness

With such unfaltering conviction, Nouwen continues to urge us all, through his writings, to openly recognize and even befriend our own mortality and broken condition. Boldly, he encourages each of us to respond to our brokenness by considering it a blessing. This counterintuitive thought captivated him each time he recalled a memorable scene from Leonard Bernstein's *Mass* in which

> the priest...is lifted up by his people...carrying a glass chalice. Suddenly, the human pyramid collapses, and the priest comes tumbling down. His...glass chalice falls to the ground and is shattered. As he walks slowly through the debris...the priest notices the broken chalice. He...says, "*I never realized that broken glass could shine so brightly*" (italics mine).

The priest's words stayed etched in Nouwen's memory, for it captured the mystery of his own existence (*LOB*:78, 82–83).

Anyone familiar with Henri Nouwen's writings cannot overlook the glaring reality that his life revolved around the mystery of the Eucharist. It was his "spiritual center of gravity," his *raison d'être*.[7] Except for rare occasions, Nouwen made it a point to celebrate holy communion every day, either by himself or with virtually anyone interested in joining him.

Brokenness as Contrition

Out of Nouwen's abiding love for and devotion to the Eucharist came some of his most enlightening meditations concerning its deeper significance. For instance, Nouwen noted that every eucharistic celebration starts with a cry for God's mercy (the Kyrie Eleison), an open acknowledgment of our own part in the brokenness of our condition.

The Kyrie Eleison represents the humble confession that "human brokenness is not a fatal condition of which we have become the sad victims, but the bitter fruit of the human choice to say 'No' to love" (*BH*:31). Far from romanticizing the revealing aspect of our woundedness and brokenness, Nouwen here exposes our coresponsibility for our fate—the reality that we have not only been sinned against by others but that we also continually sin against others.

In our day, when even the status of "legitimate" victimization has often been elevated to unreasonable heights, we need to remember that, while we are all truly victims, we remain agents first and last.[8] Generally speaking, those who view themselves merely as wounded victims are bound to demand healing and recovery; whereas people who are willing to admit to their sinful state are more likely to seek God's grace and forgiveness and follow the path of true repentance and faith. With this in view, Henri Nouwen regarded the Kyrie Eleison as emanating from a contrite and broken heart. It is a heart willing to admit "its own part in the sinfulness of the world and so has been made ready to receive God's mercy," thus making possible a thanksgiving celebration of the Eucharist along with a broken heart (*BH*:32–33).

Chosen, Blessed, Broken, Given

In yet another way of looking at the symbolic meaning of the Eucharist, we are presented a different picture of brokenness embodied in the example of Christ's own life. True to the familiar eucharistic formula invoked during holy communion, Jesus, the Bread of Life, was also "taken or chosen, blessed, broken, and given" for the world. His brokenness was meant for our wholeness (see Isa 53:5c).

Henri Nouwen's life mirrored the same eucharistic movement, albeit pale compared to Christ's but just as real: "...his life became spiritual bread and wine, body and blood, for others."[9] We are recipients today of untold blessings flowing out of Nouwen's brokenness. His own inward journey of imperfection, marked by authentic self-knowledge and self-confrontation, continues to inspire us in our own pursuit of wholeness along our own inward journey.

A Ministry of Imperfection

If the so-called inward journey is graced with elements of imperfection, so is the outward journey. This outward movement has its general focus the whole arena of ministry—reaching out to others productively.

Ministry effectiveness is about fruitfulness and definitely requires power to carry out the journey. How then do we enter this journey of ministry with power? To those who capitulate to the world's standards of power and success, Henri Nouwen's response has a strange and countercultural ring to it: It is via the ministry of imperfection—where power is shown through weakness.

Power through Weakness

God has deliberately chosen to break through human history in the person of Christ manifesting total weakness in birth and dying on the cross in voluntary powerlessness (*FWH*:33, 35). Indeed, from Henri Nouwen's viewpoint, God's way is the way of weakness. Yet this strange display of God's vulnerability was precisely what yielded fruit for our sake ultimately—salvation and eternal life for all who believe in Christ (*LS*:66).

God's unprecedented act was a downward movement, counter to self-protection and self-preservation. It was a movement from "the heights to the depth, from victory to defeat, from riches to poverty, from triumph to suffering, from life to death."[10] Based upon Christ's example, Nouwen insists that the way of the Christian minister "is not the way of upward mobility...but the way of downward mobility ending on the cross" (*INJ*:62). Whereas "[p]eople seek glory by moving upward...God reveals his glory by moving downward" (*RD*:98). Nouwen conveys the spiritual paradox of it all:

> Every time Jesus speaks about being glorified and giving glory, he always refers to his humiliation and death. It is through the way of the cross that Jesus gives glory to God, receives glory from God, and makes God's glory known to us. The glory of the resurrection can never be separated from the glory of the cross. (*RD*:98)

New Testament scholar Timothy Savage in his compelling exposition of 2 Corinthians explains that since it was in this "radical self-abnegation of the crucified Messiah that the power of God had come to its mightiest expression," it makes sense why "God had chosen to manifest his illimitable power" in human weakness. On this front, Savage directs our attention to the apostle Paul who himself affirms that only in his cruciform weakness can divine power be fully demonstrated. Furthermore, "it is precisely in such 'weakness' that true power, the power of God, becomes effective in his ministry."[11]

This is why, according to Henri Nouwen, the mystery of ministry lies in the reality that "ministers are powerless people who have nothing to boast of except their weakness," and only as we live out this powerlessness do we discover what ministry is truly about.[12] If, indeed, it is true that "[t]he cross," as Philip Sheldrake singles out, "is the greatest sign that the strength of God to transform us is shown best in the midst of our weakness (see 2 Cor 12),"[13] then it is equally true that from God's standpoint, he "has more need of our weakness than of our strength."[14]

Reduced to a simple but profound statement, the path of power is through weakness. However, this theology of weakness "claims power, God's power, the all-transforming *power of love* (italics mine)" (*FWH*:42). Again, the apostle Paul demonstrated this in his own ministry. "Like the cross of Christ, Paul's weakness is, an expression of love: 'everything is for your sake' (2 Cor 4:15)."[15] Ministry then, as a movement toward others, is powerful love in action, albeit via weakness.

At the height of his ever growing popularity, Nouwen clung to this paradoxical truth of "power through weakness" more fiercely. In response to what he believed to be a definite call from God, Nouwen made a determined choice to leave the prestigious world of academia to minister to the mentally and physically disabled people at L'Arche Daybreak (see *RP*:xviii–xxv). There, Nouwen experienced firsthand what it meant to truly minister in love and power through his own weakness as he took care of a severely handicapped young man named Adam. Never did Nouwen have any tinge of regret for his decision to settle in L'Arche. From Nouwen's perspective, in his weakness "[Adam] became a unique instrument of God's grace" and a "revelation of Christ among us" (*A*:30).

In summary, the outward journey Nouwen embarked on has to do with a ministry of imperfection in which weakness forms the basis for fruitfulness. Its real power, ironically, is one derived through powerlessness.

A Theology of Imperfection

Alongside psychological wholeness stands its integral counterpart—spiritual wholeness, or what theologians prefer to call holiness. Others equate the concept with that of Christian perfection. The process leading up to that ideal is identified with the theological idea of sanctification or growth in holiness.

Just as there are varying perspectives concerning psychological wholeness, so are there competing notions about the concept of holiness. A wide assortment of spiritual pathways has been outlined by Christians representing various theological persuasions from Reformed to Keswick to charismatic, validating the existence of what biblical theologian Donald Alexander calls "the riddle of sanctification."[16] Conflicting views about the spiritual life are many, and they can sometimes be thoroughly confusing. The subjects of conversion, growth, change, and transformation have always been regular features of debate among Bible scholars and theologians.

In an unquestionably sincere attempt to promote a life of holiness, many have taken extreme theological positions that sometimes border on the triumphal, if not perfectionist. Most, if not all, advocates of these views tend to turn a blind eye to the primacy of the cross as the compelling symbol of authentic Christian experience. A robust theology of suffering seems absent in the overall spiritual equation.

Triumphalism, of course, wears many faces. It is a familiar fixture in much of the so-called victorious life teaching so widespread today. Many, for example, commonly construe the *normal* Christian life as "one of uniform, sustained victory over known sin."[17] Sincere proponents of this idea are by no means teaching sinless perfection in this life. Such an overemphasis on victory, however, will not only potentially blind us to the glaring reality of living in a fallen world but can also promote an unhealthy denial of the lingering effects of sin in our daily lives. In actual experience, many will openly testify that "growing closer to God involves a deepening recognition that we are far from perfect...and that holiness is more normally "connected with failure and the acceptance of failure."[18]

Anglican theologian J. I. Packer warns that "any idea of getting beyond conflict...in our pursuit of holiness in this life is an escapist dream that can only have disillusioning and demoralizing effect on us."[19] Author Ron Julian reinforces Packer's sentiment by further pointing out that the idea of triumphalism "can put the struggling believer in a painful and unnecessary bind" by being labeled "*abnormal* for something that is *normal*."[20]

Earlier in the discussion of the upward or Godward journey we touched on communion, which deals with our ongoing pursuit of holiness or union with God. We noted the primary vehicle driving this communion, which is prayer. It would be a mistake to think that communing in and through prayer is a purely interior matter. Prayer, if it is genuine, propels us to move out into the exterior reality of things. Henri Nouwen states, "When we pray we are never satisfied with the world of here and now, and are constantly striving to realize the new world" (*OH*:73). Moreover, he shows how, in prayer, our spiritual attentiveness naturally grows:

> The closer we come to God in prayer, the more we become aware of...the presence of [God's] gifts in the midst of our pains and sorrows. The mystery of the spiritual life is that many events, people, and situations that for a long time seemed to inhibit our way to God become ways of our being united more deeply with him.[21]

Prayer itself, Nouwen informs us, "does not keep pain away from us." It is tantamount to an illusion to entertain the idea that "reaching out to God will free us from pain and suffering" (*RO*:150). Communion with God is a communion through suffering.

Communion through Suffering

Henri Nouwen declared with certainty: "There is no journey to God outside of the journey that Jesus made" (*RPS*:56)—and that includes the inevitable way of suffering. Our communion with our God, however intimate, is not without its share of pain and sorrow. Nouwen himself admitted to being baffled by this seemingly contradictory reality:

> The experience of God's presence is not void of pain. But the pain is so deep that you do not want to miss it since it is in this pain that the joy of God's presence can be tasted. This seems close to nonsense…hard to capture within the limits of human understanding. (*GD*:142)

A somewhat similar sense is enigmatically depicted in the famous *Icon of the Trinity* painted by the Russian iconographer Andrei Rublev in 1425. Henri Nouwen utilized this classic work of art for his own personal meditation. Rublev's painting portrays in exquisitely detailed strokes the circle of communion existing within the Triune God and the open invitation for all of us to participate in this intimate communion.

During one of his intense meditative moments, Nouwen was led to conclude that the open space in the lower middle portion of the icon signifies the narrow road paved with suffering. In Nouwen's inspired interpretation, the trinitarian figures reveal a melancholic type of beauty that seems to evoke Jesus' penetrating question: "'Can you drink the cup?'"[22] One gathers that the invitation to commune with the reality of God the Trinity also consists of a call to fellowship with the reality of suffering.

Such beckoning images help us recall that communion with God involves being in union with the God of suffering (see Isa 53:3b). In God's economy, uniting with him means that we take on a share of Christ's sufferings (cf. Phil 3:10). That the privilege of being one with God has an accompanying cost is laid out for us by the apostle Paul (who was no stranger to suffering himself) in his letter to the Philippian believers: "For he has graciously granted you the privilege not only of believing in Christ, but of suffering for him as well" (Phil 1:29).

On various occasions, Jesus foretold his own suffering and death to convey to his disciples that "a person who wants to lead a spiritual life cannot do so without the prospect of suffering and death" (*LM*:29). Yet in spite of the inescapable reality that suffering is certain to accompany the spiritual journey, many Christians avoid experiencing it at all costs. Not only do some succumb to a distorted view of suffering, but they also seem to drug it out of existence altogether. Others insist on imagining a suffering-free existence that simply does not exist.

Henri Nouwen did not want anything to do with such an unrealistic—short of an illusional—outlook on the Christian life. Not a slightest tissue of triumphalism resided in his bones. His theological anthropology prevented him from giving in to such an idealistic propensity. On the contrary, he was a consummate realist concerning the human condition. Nouwen did not seem to have trouble accepting our residual fallenness as a factor in the suffering that has now become our inevitable lot.[23] As one whose ceaseless struggle proved to be the bane of his existence, Henri Nouwen knew suffering intimately. By any measure, he suffered well himself.[24]

French philosopher and mystic Simone Weil espoused the belief that while Christianity does not provide any "supernatural remedy for suffering," Christians can still maximize "a supernatural use for it."[25] Most of us, however, tend to sidestep the prospect of learning from our experience of suffering by holding on to anything that can alleviate our struggle as quickly as possible. Henri Nouwen exposes our natural tendencies: "We…like easy victories: growth without crisis, healing without pains, the resurrection without the cross."[26]

Henri Nouwen, as his intimate diaries bear witness, fought against such tendencies himself. Yet despite the agony involved, he hardly recoiled from the astringent nature of suffering. Nouwen is thus in a credible position to instruct us that "when we learn to move through suffering, rather than avoid it, then we greet it differently. We become willing to let it teach us. We even begin to see how God can use it for some larger end."[27] Henri Nouwen lived well the truth of his own words. It was said of him that his own protracted anguish in life was what actually "fueled his genius."[28]

True to everyone's journey, "suffering is the kiln through which we all must…pass."[29] Henri Nouwen's life merely reinforces what the New Testament discloses—that the actual path leading to glory is strewn all over by an abundance of suffering.

Suffering as a Prelude to Glory

Against the imposing nature of suffering, Henri Nouwen poses to us the right question to ponder. For him, it is "not how to avoid loss and make it not happen, but how to choose it as a passage, as an exodus to greater life and freedom" (*FWH*:137). In *Can You Drink the Cup?*, which Henri Nouwen penned during his sabbatical year just before he passed away, he relied on the metaphor of the "cup" as the central focus and controlling imagery by which he summed up the essence of the spiritual life and what it means to follow Christ. Nouwen specifically addressed the serious challenge of drinking the cup of life containing not only salvation, blessings, and joy, but also sorrow. He drew from the example of Christ, who chose not to do away with the cup of suffering but willingly submitted himself instead to the will of his Father, "the lover of his wounded heart" (see Matt 26:39). In Christ's life as in his death we discover the greatest of mystery that defies logic.

> Jesus' unconditional yes to his Father had empowered him to drink his cup, not in passive resignation but with the full knowledge that the hour of his death would also be the hour of his glory. His yes made his surrender a creative act, an act that could bear much fruit. Instead of a final irrevocable end, his death became the beginning of a new life. Indeed, his yes enabled him to trust fully in the rich harvest the dying grain would yield. (*CYD*:50)

Christ drank deeply and willingly from the cup of his own life, and it brought him "freedom, glory, and wholeness" (*CYD*:88). Jesus' moment of death on the cross turned out to be "his life's greatest moment, because there his life became the most fruitful one in all history" (*FWH*:144). What this emphasizes is that what was true for Christ is likewise true for all of us—at least as a biblical principle. If "communion with Jesus means becoming like him...lead[ing] us to a new realm of being...usher[ing] us into the Kingdom" (*BH*:74), then suffering is the expected pathway to the said Kingdom.

As followers of the crucified Savior, all Christians are to be ready to carry their own crosses as they go about the way of Jesus.

The Jewish-born Carmelite sister Edith Stein placed the symbol of the cross within the framework of the "Paschal Mystery of Christ," our share of which, she said, "destines us to suffer and to die with him, but also to arise." When our faith focuses and expands on the mystery's positive vision, it "opens for us the stream of his life and the beginning of future glory."[30]

Human suffering, when seen as an integral part of the journey toward the full realization of our humanity, can thus be a gateway to joy instead of an obstacle. This was what the two downcast travelers walking on the road to Emmaus realized when their attention was arrested by the "stranger's" revealing question: "Was it not necessary that the Messiah should suffer these things and then enter into his glory?" (Luke 24:26).

Henri Nouwen points out that when Jesus raised the piercing question "Are you able to drink the cup that I am about to drink?" to James and John, the sons of Zebedee (Matt 20:22b), he knew that both for him and for them, suffering was the absolute route to glory. Too, Nouwen is convinced that all of us can decide to drink our own cup of life with the deep conviction that by doing so, "we will find our true freedom" and "discover that the cup of sorrow and joy we are drinking is the cup of salvation" (*CYD*:83; 48–49).

The comforting truth is that our intimate communion with God is what enables and sustains us as we keep drinking our cup. All this constitutes what it really means to follow Christ and to conform to the example of his life. The apostle Paul makes it plain that conformity to Christ essentially involves a present and a future thrust. The present one concerns our gradual growth in Christlikeness based upon the ministry of the Spirit in our life (2 Cor 3:18). The future one points with finality to our complete sanctification and is directly equivalent to our glorification as believers, when at last, we will no longer "fall short of the glory of God" (cf. Rom 3:23).

It is crucial to understand that the present conformity has as its primary context the suffering described in Romans 8:17–23. Growing in Christ's likeness here and now means fellowshipping with him in suffering prior to fellowshipping with him in glory. Therefore, for the time being, as David Peterson urges us, "we must be content...to share visibly in the pattern of Christ's death rather than in the pattern of his glory."[31] Suffering is the necessary prelude to the future glory awaiting us all.

Our Hope of Final Glory

Our communion with God involves a journey of which the final consummation is glory—also referred to as *deification, beatific vision,* or *full union with God.* The one sure thing the Scripture promises all of us is this: "When [Christ] is revealed, we will be like him, for we will see him as he is" (1 John 3:2b). To quote Saint Augustine's expression of great awe: "Our seeing then, Lord, will be the vision of you as you are, but this is not granted to us yet."[32] For this present time, while still on the road to glory, we look ahead with hope and exercise faith. With a calm sense of preparedness, Henri Nouwen could say:

> I know that the longer I live, the more suffering I will see and...the more sorrow I will be asked to live. But it is this deep human sorrow that unites my wounded heart with the heart of humanity. It is in this mystery of union in suffering that hope is hidden.[33]

With a comforting note of assurance, Nouwen adds: "The great secret in life is that suffering, which often seems to be so unbearable, can become...a source of new life and new hope" (*LM*:33).

Far from mere theorizing, Henri Nouwen spoke of the vitality of this hope from personal experience. Michael Ford attests that "[b]y embracing his own loneliness, depression, and struggles in faith, Henri Nouwen, too, trusted that he would find light and hope in the center of his pain."[34] Nouwen himself testified to a friend during one of the most difficult periods of his life: "Never have I felt so strongly how great pain and anguish can lead to new life, new hope, new courage."[35] From Nouwen's own testimony— and to be sure, from many others' as well—notwithstanding what is already a trite saying, suffering does serve a definite purpose. For one thing, the very experience of suffering itself enables us to grasp the living reality of hope.

As God's children, we are coheirs with Christ, but as Nouwen points out, this full honor also includes the full pain. Often, we forget that if "we are willing to share in Christ's suffering, we also will share in his glory" (*BJ*: June 6). There will surely come a day when all suffering will cease and the whole of creation will experience renewal. Henri Nouwen allows us to get a glimpse via Paul of God's grand vision of his redemptive work through Christ:

> Paul sees the whole created order as a woman groaning in labor, waiting eagerly to give birth to a new life. He writes, "It was not for its own purposes that creation had frustration imposed on it, but for the purposes of him who imposed it—with the intention that the whole creation itself might be freed from its slavery to corruption and brought into the same glorious freedom as the children of God" (Romans 8:20–21). All that God has created will be lifted up into God's glory. (*BJ*:December 8)

Despite our share of life's hardships, eternal glory waits in the horizon—and it outweighs all the burdens we can ever experience this side of heaven. Keeping this in mind can motivate us to live with expectant hope as we prepare ourselves to go home in glory.

Perfection through Imperfection

Henri Nouwen's integrated pursuit of the spiritual journey toward a life of wholeness and holiness—*inward, outward*, and *upward*—does constitute inherent imperfections: psychological, ministerial, and theological. All that to point that the journey to perfection is indeed through imperfection—the summary statement that captures the focal theme of this book.

Holiness and Perfection

One nagging question, however, continues to confront many of us: Does not the Bible issue a clear command for us to be *holy* and *perfect*? Few verses in the New Testament have generated as much confusion and misunderstanding as Matthew 5:48: "Be perfect, therefore, as your heavenly Father is perfect." Focusing on this single verse without the benefit of situating it within its larger context often triggers a skeptical response, even from the most sincere believer of the Bible: Could Jesus really mean exactly that?

When comprehended in its right context, this verse presents a completely different picture that can assuage the anxiety usually brought on by a cursory reading of the text. To begin with, Jesus' call to perfection recorded in Matthew 5:48, which occurs in the middle of the famous Sermon on the Mount (Matt 5–7), has as its preceding context his clear command to love and pray for one's enemies. Exercising this kind of love proves that we, indeed, belong to God (the God who "makes his sun rise on the evil and on the good" [Matt 5:45]).

The passage is essentially saying that if we are to be like God, who shows no favoritism but loves everyone alike, we are expected to love all kinds of people, the unlovable included. Taken as a whole then, the passage is an unambiguous call to exhibit perfect love—the kind that is expressed even to those who do not reciprocate it. What Jesus specifies here pertains to an all-encompassing type of love. The parallel verse found in Luke 6:36 ("Be merciful, just as your Father is merciful") confirms this: We are "to love even our enemies with the merciful, the inclusive love of God."[36] In short, we are all admonished to love unconditionally.

In light of this interpretation, Jesus' teachings contained in this popular sermon—including the climactic call to perfection in Matthew 5:48—are not to be construed as "impossible moral ideals, or idealistic moral perfection, but practical deeds of love toward enemies, including prayer for them."[37] Thus, far from "advocating the pursuit of perfection as a striving for individual moral perfection," the Matthean verse actually calls for "a life-long stretching of one's capacity to love as God does."[38] Perfection then is really all about love.

Interestingly, this coincides with what John Wesley generally understood perfection to be: "...perfection for Wesley meant nothing more or less than the scriptural injunction to love all, including our enemies."[39] Wesley equated the idea of holiness with perfection, which he defined as "the *perfect* love of God and our neighbor reigning over *all* other loves and interests."[40]

Thus, in the Wesleyan understanding of what true perfection entails, a careful delineation is made: Perfection is about complete freedom to love, not necessarily freedom from flaws. For one thing, the Greek word used in the Matthean text, *teleios*, has more to do with the idea of "completeness than [with] freedom from fault or error."[41] A thing is said to be *teleios* "if it realizes the purpose for which it was planned or created."[42] Therefore, if we are growing in love, we are moving toward completeness, wholeness and integration—toward "perfection" in holiness, to which we are ultimately called.

How do we then make the journey toward wholeness and holiness, toward this state called perfection? Henri Nouwen's documented experiences richly illustrate a paradoxical answer: The movement to perfection takes place in the context of spiritual imperfection.

As Thomas Merton stated: Spiritual perfection "is attained not by those who have superhuman strength but by those who, though weak and defective in themselves, trust perfectly in the love of God."[43] In this case, Henri Nouwen is the embodiment of such an experiential reality. His own imperfect journey substantiates it.

Spiritual Journey of Imperfection

Henri Nouwen's journey was littered with bits and pieces of the realities of imperfection. Nouwen never entertained the illusion that the spiritual journey consisted of neat stages. As veteran spiritual director Wilkie Au describes it, the journey "is not an easy-flowing straight line, but more of a serpentine path of ups and downs."[44] Spiritual life does not proceed in a linear manner, as our waking experience proves.

While recognizing that many great saints in the past have tried systematizing spiritual experiences into various phases, levels, or stages, Henri Nouwen preferred not to be governed by the whole notion of measurement and degrees when addressing the life of the Spirit (*RO*:17). Indeed, much of medieval Christianity seemed to exhibit a certain fixation on spiritual progress as a hierarchical concept. Evidence of this is seen in the well-known imagery of the "ladder" and "ascent" as an approximate portrayal of the spiritual journey to God.[45]

Franciscan priest Richard Rohr does not mince words in decrying "ascent theology" not only as problematic, but also as unsupported by Scripture. Instead of the language of ascent, the

Bible, Rohr insists, fosters the idea of descent—featuring the postures of abandonment and humble surrender. To Rohr, far from eradicating struggles and failures, the way to perfection necessarily includes such elements of imperfection.[46] The focus is not so much on measurable progress or spiritual advancement but more on the experience of inner transformation despite—and perhaps because of—imperfection.

Theologian Charles Ringma underscores the fact that the rhythms of our spiritual journey do not necessarily follow our physical and social development patterns. Ringma comprehends it this way:

> Physically and emotionally we grow from childhood into adulthood. And unless we are psychologically or socially underdeveloped, we leave that childhood phase behind us. It is not quite like that with our spiritual growth. We are encouraged to grow from "babes in Christ" into spiritual maturity. But [it] does not necessarily mean strength, competence and independence. *It does not mean that we have arrived* (emphasis mine).[47]

Such is the nature of our journey. We are always in the process of "arriving." Philip Sheldrake states that "the most dangerous spirituality is that of possession—being in a 'state of perfection' or even conceiving of perfection as a state at all." With stern conviction he issues this caution:

> The moment that we feel that we have arrived, are complete, or indeed that there is a potential moment when such will be the case (when we will change from movement to mere maintenance) we are furthest from God. Holiness...has a great deal to do with a realisation and acceptance of imperfection and even failure and of the need for continual conversion. Holiness is a process, a continual movement towards God.[48]

With characteristic honesty, Henri Nouwen was one of the first to confess: "I am unable to say that I have arrived; I never will in this life..." (*RPS*:17). Along with the great apostle Paul he could say, "...not that I have already obtained this, or have already been made perfect, but I press on..." (Phil 3:12NIV).

Nouwen gave this warning: "Those who think they have arrived, have lost their way. Those who think they have reached their goal, have missed it" (*GD*:133). Nouwen never hesitated to expose his own spiritual inabilities, even if by doing so it would seem, on the surface, to neutralize the power of the gospel that he sought to proclaim. On the contrary, instead of jeopardizing his witness, Nouwen's credibility increases even as he "becomes a mirror for all of us Christians who daily fail to be 'perfect as [our] heavenly Father is perfect.'"[49]

By now it is clear that "the spiritual journey for Nouwen was never about perfection, but about struggling to live in a deep and meaningful relationship with God that would bear fruit in the lives of others."[50] Popular writer Mike Yaconelli articulated this truth so pointedly:

> Spirituality is not about perfection; it is about connection. The way of the spiritual life begins where we are now in the mess of our lives. Accepting the reality of our broken, flawed lives is the beginning of spirituality not because the spiritual life will remove our flaws but because we let go of seeking perfection and, instead, seek God, the one who is present in the tangledness of our lives.[51]

As most of us realize through our daily experience, life is not without interruptions, displacements, detours, and all kinds of impediments. Sadly, many sincere Christians are erroneously "led to expect a steady spiritual ascent" when in reality, "life with God often turns out to involve far more struggle and ambiguity than is sometimes advertised."[52]

For some of us, ambiguity is intolerable because we tend to associate it with the state of being in the dark. Its unsettling effect makes us want to get away from it, in whatever form that escape takes. But as Archbishop Rowan Williams is keen on pointing out, "To want to escape the 'night' and the costly struggles with doubt and vacuity is to seek another God from the one who speaks in and as Jesus crucified."[53] In our spiritual life we are bound to struggle with this disturbing sense of "unknowing" and "unseeing," which serves as a constant reminder of our human and spiritual limitations.

The truth of the matter is that "spiritual limitations inhere in the human condition."[54] All of us, without exception, struggle with our experience of finitude. We simply do not have what it takes to make life work for us. Besides this, God himself has deliberately subjected the whole creation to futility and frustration (Rom 8:20). Consequently, life as we know it is far from orderly; it is now marked by chaos. It is definitely a mess but nonetheless a "blessed mess" because hope does not cease to exist even in the midst of a spiritually polluted state.[55]

Despite this seemingly gloomy scenario we find ourselves in, we still have solid reasons to hope as believers. Henri Nouwen often rehearsed in his heart that living the spiritual life necessitates the inner disposition of expectancy, of eager waiting and hoping (GD:133). At the same time, we would also do well to heed Reinhold Niebuhr's urging to exercise dynamic restraint in expressing our Christian hope because "faith must admit 'that it doth not yet appear what we shall be.'"[56]

Henri Nouwen was always one to advocate a more realistic view of the spiritual life. To this end, he espoused a theology and spirituality of imperfection that featured the recurring themes of struggle, suffering, powerlessness, and weakness. Nouwen was by no means the only one to subscribe to this brand of spirituality. Saints in times past have long embraced it as they did their own humanness. It is, as authors Ernest Kurtz and Katherine Ketcham eagerly point out, a spirituality that is thousands of years old and "one that is more sensitive to earthly concerns than to heavenly hopes." It is the kind that has more to do with "the reality of the here and now, with living humanly as one is" and therefore, one that "involves how to live with imperfection." Kurtz and Ketcham masterfully expound on this thought:

> The core paradox that underlies spirituality is the haunting sense of incompleteness....For to be human is to be incomplete, yet yearn for completion; it is to be uncertain, yet long for certainty; to be imperfect, yet long for perfection; to be broken, yet crave for wholeness. All these yearnings remain necessarily unsatisfied...because we are imperfectly human—or better, because we are perfectly human, which is to say humanly imperfect.[57]

The early saints all seemed to embrace a spirituality of imperfection that was "far removed from the schemes of spiritual exercises and the guides to the higher reaches of 'contemplation' that have come to be the stock in trade of spiritual writers."[58] This same spirituality of imperfection was what Henri Nouwen fully embodied—theologically and practically—in both his life and ministry.

In his struggle-ridden existence and virtual experience of woundedness, at times accompanied by periods of darkness, Henri Nouwen exemplified imperfection. Yet in the midst of it all, Nouwen possessed a spiritual wisdom that ensured that imperfection did not become the ultimate overriding theme of his life as much as his courage and willingness to confront imperfection in light of the power of the Gospel.

Time and again, Henri Nouwen's transparent experience bore out the truth that only in the full awareness of limitations and weaknesses does one discover God's ample supply of power and grace. Herein lies the blessed side of a genuinely imperfect existence.[59] In the final section that follows, we shall see this truth exemplified in greater detail in Henri Nouwen's life experience.

CHAPTER FIVE

A Perfect Example of Imperfection

In this final chapter we will examine the counterintuitive type of spirituality Henri Nouwen personified before the watching world. What others consider a spiritual liability has turned out to be the genius behind Nouwen's authentic spirituality: its glaring imperfection. Nouwen represents a perfect paradigm of imperfection. Embodied through his life are the sobering realities of an imperfect life: as a *restless seeker*, as a *wounded healer*, and as a *faithful struggler*.

Henri Nouwen was an inconsolably restless soul for much of his entire earthly journey, but no doubt a passionate seeker of himself, of other people, and of his God. Noted for being a severely wounded person, he was nonetheless a highly effective healer of other souls. Lastly, Nouwen was a perennial struggler through all of life's battles while remaining a faithful fighter until the very end. His disordered existence, if nothing else, speaks powerfully of the sacramental blessings of an imperfect life.

A Restless Seeker

On this issue of restlessness, journalist Philip Yancey offers an intriguing answer to a question he himself raises: "Living as resident aliens in a strange land, citizens of a secret kingdom, what other kind of peace should we expect? In this world, restlessness, and not contentment is a sign of health."[1] If this is true, then Henri Nouwen conducted a sane existence since his was undeniably full of restless longing—both inward and outward.

Certainly, a streak of restlessness resides in all of us. With Henri Nouwen, though, he not only possessed a restless heart; he seemed thoroughly motivated by it. Out of the depths of his being constantly overflowed boundless energy. Nouwen's unrelenting search encompassed "everything within and just beyond reach: God, himself, the people and the world around him."[2] Waves of restlessness found their way in both the inward and the outward longings of Nouwen's heart. He was restless to find himself, to seek after God, to do something for the world.

An Abiding Restlessness Within

As might be expected, the beginning point of Nouwen's seeking was always his own heart: "My lonely self...should be my first source of search and research," Nouwen confirmed (*RO*:29). An ardent seeker of himself, Nouwen, without hesitation, embarked on an inward journey to his deepest self. There within its hidden corners, he paid close attention to the irregular beatings of his heart.

It was in his interiority where Henri Nouwen attempted to make sense of the lingering contradictions of his restless existence. Out of his interior excavation he emerged at times a more hopeful soul, more in touch with his own longing. If we but start listening more carefully to our restless hearts, Nouwen claimed,

> we may start to sense that in the midst of our sadness there is joy, that in the midst of our fears there is peace, that in the midst of our greediness there is possibility of compassion and that indeed in the midst of our irking loneliness we can find the beginnings of a quiet solitude. (*RO*:36)

The only problem was that the same hope on which he banked to sustain him usually ended up getting dashed as quickly as he latched on to it. Much to his dismay, he confessed one time: "My own restlessness...[has] made me flee solitude as soon as I have found it" (*GG*:1). A confession of this sort reeks of the kind of tension Nouwen, in all likelihood, must have dealt with time and again.

Longings and Desires

Just what was this restlessness about Nouwen? In his case—as in all of us—it was predictably freighted with both positive and negative forces. In Nouwen we find a subtle overlap between pure longing and imperfect desire, an almost paradoxical interplay of darkness and light, altogether lodged in his complex personality.

On one hand, Nouwen's restlessness no doubt became the driving force behind some of his most productive output as a creative writer. His colorful journals alone—composed in the midst of restless searching and wandering—stand as rich evidence of Nouwen's reflective genius, revealing no less his genuine desire to seek the most intimate communion with God possible. On the other hand, it was Nouwen's seemingly uncontainable restlessness that likewise dragged into focus the rather naïve and erroneous perspectives behind certain calculated moves of his.

On June 1, 1974, Henri Nouwen began his seven-month commitment to live as a monk at the Abbey of the Genesee in upstate New York. The decision came about after many years of restless searching until he felt ready to confront his fragmented self within the regulated confines of a Trappist monastery. Coming out of his experience more than half a year later, Nouwen looked back and with searing honesty admitted to having nourished the hidden illusion that seven months of Trappist life could end his inner turmoil. In the conclusion of his Genesee diary, Nouwen bemoaned: "Somehow I had expected that my restlessness would turn into quietude, my tensions into a peaceful life-style [*sic*], and my ambiguities and ambivalences into a single-minded commitment to God" (*GD*:217).

About his genuine desire to be single-minded, to will one thing, there was hardly any question. There had been instances, however, when Nouwen basically sabotaged his own determination to focus by allowing his compulsions to overpower him. At one point when he gained more freedom to overcome some of his warped tendencies, Nouwen recounted a fairly common scenario in his life with his trusted spiritual guide at Genesee, Father John Eudes Bamberger:

Normally, when I receive many letters I complain that I am too busy, and when I receive none I complain about lack of attention; when I work a lot I complain about lack of time to study and pray, when I work little I feel guilty for not making a contribution. (*GD*:202)

This conflicting profile of Nouwen is really not that unusual at all. Many of us probably see our own restless versions of ourselves through Nouwen's pictured condition—including the way he indulged in what has come to be notoriously labeled the "narcotic of busyness."

Busyness as Restless Distraction

As most of his journal entries reveal, it was typical for Nouwen to drown himself in a flurry of activities or overextend himself to multiple and even simultaneous tasks, often oblivious of his own limits. If it were completely left up to him, Nouwen could have so readily responded to all the endless invitations coming from various quarters to do this and to do that. To begin with, Nouwen usually found it difficult to say no to any and every opportunity that regularly came his way. He was one always eager to please everyone. Fortunately, Nouwen was surrounded by a few caring friends who tried to help him regulate and manage his often overcrowded schedule.

Long before *multitasking* emerged as a buzzword, Nouwen was already heavily engaging in it as though it was second nature. It is probably not a stretch of imagination to say that he literally lived out the meaning of the term *multitasking*—and to a large extent, with negative repercussions. Nouwen's penchant for spreading himself thin, along with his obsessive-compulsive behavior and "workaholic" drive, all seemed to conspire in bringing out the unhealthy side of his restless maneuvers.

Busyness became a cheap distraction to keep Nouwen's depressive tendencies at bay (*SJ*:101). As long as he was preoccupied with writing projects and speaking engagements, Nouwen did not have to face his insecurities directly nor wallow in his awful feeling of aloneness. Leading a busy life was perhaps a more convenient way for him to cope with his persistent state of unsettledness. It appeared as though Nouwen was so wired to function in nothing but overdrive position that anything less would have fueled more restlessness inside him.

Nouwen's Balancing Act

With the kind of hectic pace that Henri Nouwen led, he could have so easily run out of gas, so to speak. But he never did. That was because, even with his sometimes insane schedule, he actually never had to run on empty. Nouwen knew the secret of solitude. More importantly, he practiced it. He had a solid anchor, a vital connection with God that was sustained by the discipline of silence and solitude, a practiced discipline that kept Nouwen intact and served to strengthen his inner man.

The only irony is—if one could call it that—Henri Nouwen felt its need as much as he craved for an ongoing social interaction and active engagement with all sorts of live events, activities, and friends. Positively speaking, the idea of creating and experiencing a real sense of community ranked uppermost on Nouwen's priority list. He loved people and simply could not live without them.

Evidently, interacting with people—and Nouwen had tons of friends he loved engaging with—was just as equally important for him as communing with God in silence and solitude. As such, Nouwen's staunch but oftentimes frustrating attempt to balance his two passions, solitude and community, only exacerbated his already existing struggle with restlessness.

A Restless Search for God

However else one might interpret it, behind all of Henri Nouwen's restlessness lay an authentic desire to seek after God. Even his inner search for himself pointed to a much deeper longing to be in union with God. Nouwen spoke of his desire to be with Jesus as his "oldest and deepest desire," which he had had since "the first moment of [his] consciousness."[3] It could be said that his heart, like the psalmist, truly panted after God. Nouwen sought God like one who could hardly wait to go home in glory.

During one particularly rare moment in his life, amidst a close brush with death itself, Nouwen received a foretaste of what it must be like to experience a homecoming with Jesus. This sort of mystical vision occurred in the face of a serious operation he was about to undergo as a result of a road accident in 1989.

Nouwen described the experience poignantly:

> I felt his presence in a most tangible way, as if my whole life had come together and I was being enfolded in love. The homecoming had a real quality of return, a return to the womb of God. The God who had fashioned me in secret and molded me in the depths of the earth, the God who had knitted me together in my mother's womb, was calling me back after a long journey and wanted to receive me as someone who had become child enough to be loved as a child. (*BM*:49–50)

In 1996, some seven years after this exalted event, a massive heart attack snuffed out Nouwen's life. His vision finally turned into reality. Nouwen was ushered to a *real* homecoming with God in which he became restless no more.

Deep within, Henri Nouwen always knew his true dwelling place to be with God. But before reaching his final resting place, Nouwen often found himself roaming around, desperately seeking love. Owning up to it, he confessed: "I am the prodigal son every time I search for unconditional love where it cannot be found" (*RPS*:43).

In a written prayer to Jesus, Nouwen uttered the same familiar refrain: "I know where I can safely dwell. I know where I can listen to the voice of love. But still I am restless, searching for what only you can give" (*HSH*:51). One senses the obvious tension expressed by Nouwen's sentiments. Still, they bleed with profuse honesty.

The Story of Our Lives

Even with such candid admission about the wanderings of his soul, Henri Nouwen was certainly not just speaking for himself. He was giving voice to the familiar story of many of us. If we but think for a moment and reflect upon our own life, chances are, we can identify a common pattern that characterizes our natural propensities when it comes to our relationship with God.

In this regard, an Old Testament passage comes to mind. God has spoken to the prophet Jeremiah, saying, "...for my people have committed two evils: they have forsaken me, the fountain of living water, and dug out cisterns for themselves, cracked cisterns that can hold no water" (Jer 2:13). What a graphic image mirroring many of our own foolish moves to find fulfillment in life! Don't we find ourselves playing out that scene many times over? Our versions may be different but they all reveal one thing.

It is true that God created us with a thirst that only he can quench. Instead of coming to God, though, we wander elsewhere in our attempt to satisfy our longings through certain people and other things like our job, our achievements, our material possessions, etcetera. But, as the cliché goes, we merely end up "looking for the right thing in all the wrong places."

Resting in the Love of God

Was it not St. Augustine who said that God himself has put inside us a deep yearning for communion with him and that our heart will remain restless until it has been fully united in God? True, God has not yet completely filled up the void inside each of us. But someday, he definitely will. And we can count on it.

Our present circumstances, including our restless meandering, do not change the fact that ultimately, we find our secure home only in God. It is precisely this security that provides hope for us to move forward in the face of our yet unfulfilled longing. But what is really involved in that longing? In short, what exactly are we yearning to experience?

Could it be that we can only find complete rest in the deep knowledge and experience of God's eternal love? That the ultimate rest our hearts are longing for has to do with the final enjoyment of God himself who is love? Thus, to be at home with God is to be at home with the presence of love enveloping us for all eternity.

According to Nouwen, however, finding the treasure of God's love without yet having the readiness to fully possess it is enough to make one restless. Yet he hastened to qualify that it is "the restlessness of the search for God....the way to holiness....[and] the journey to the place where [one] can rest" (*IVL*:112). Was

Nouwen himself not yet fully ready to embrace the love of God, which promised to be the "secret" that would put his restless heart to complete rest? By Nouwen's admission, he continued to struggle, inclining his ear to hear the voice of love to which he became deaf at times—that same voice that kept assuring him that he was indeed the beloved of God (*RPS*:39).

Henri Nouwen's unreadiness to be enveloped by God's love completely is not a unique struggle at all. It is the same thing that I suspect all of us wrestle with again and again. Though the rhetoric of God's love regularly peppers our Christian lingo, I doubt that very many actually experience its reality moment-by-moment. But that should not stop any of us from relentlessly pursuing its reality. Doing so actively involves a continual choice to trust that God is exactly who he claims to be: a loving God. But also, that we too are exactly who he says we are: beloved of God. The struggle to embrace both truths is sometimes what arouses a deeper restlessness of spirit within us all.

A Never-Ending Search

During his fifty-fourth birthday, six months before he finally settled into his newfound "home" at L'Arche Daybreak, Henri Nouwen reflected upon his life and the restlessness that still beset him.

> Looking back, I realize that I am still struggling with the same problems I had on the day of my ordination twenty-nine years ago....[V]ery little, if anything has changed with regard to my search for inner unity and peace. I am still the restless, nervous, intense, distracted, and impulse-driven person I was when I set out on this spiritual journey. (*RD*:127)

Nouwen's open confession that he still was not all that "together" after all those years can seem at first anything but encouraging. Yet for many of us, Nouwen's honesty secretly consoles us if we are but open to admit it. For he seems just like us really, pathetically slow in terms of spiritual progress. Yet despite such a snail's pace, Nouwen never put a stop to his earnest seeking.

Seeking beyond and outside of Himself

Of equal importance to Henri Nouwen's inward longing to find himself and enter into union with God was his outward longing to be a significant player in what God was doing in the world. Such was palpably evident in Nouwen's concern for peace and justice and in his burning desire to be in close solidarity with the poor and those living on the margins of society.

Henri Nouwen grew more restless as he witnessed firsthand the ugly faces of oppression and injustice. As a result of his six-month sojourn in Bolivia and Peru in 1981 and subsequent trips to Mexico, Nicaragua, and Honduras in 1983, the fight for human dignity figured more prominently in his lectures and writings (see G!).[4] Nouwen's exposure to Latin America eventually led him on a sort of a "reverse mission" in which he took upon himself the role of a spokesperson for the South to the North. This he voluntarily did in order to heighten public awareness about the injustices occurring in the third world.

On a much deeper level, however, Henri Nouwen's active involvement in Latin America was not simply about a genuine concern for justice. Underneath it all lay his silent clamor for stability—for a sense of "home" in which he could settle.

Nouwen's incurable restlessness—inward and outward—not only kept him on the move in order to advance, but it also prompted him to seek a place to retreat. Between the freedom of movement and the prospect of stability, Nouwen seemed often torn. In many ways, his dilemma captures the inevitable tension between stability and mobility in everyone's journey.

Stability and Mobility

As already alluded to, behind Henri Nouwen's constant mobility—his seemingly endless searching and exploring—was a real ache for stability. Elsewhere Nouwen declared: "When God has become our shepherd, our refuge, our fortress, then we can reach out to him in the midst of a broken world and feel *at home while still on the way*" (RO:148).

This sure-sounding statement is but one of Nouwen's many pronouncements which, even he admitted, were easier said than done. Nouwen, like every seeker, had to grapple with the inherent tension between the dynamics of stability and mobility, which, as we shall find out, are tied directly to the intriguing notion of "place."

The Role of Place

Many of us are perhaps not even fully conscious about the significant role of place both in sustaining stability as well as promoting mobility within the context of our social and spiritual formation. Place fascinatingly goes beyond the mere concept of physical or social location; it pertains as much to the geography of our spirit.

Place and Spirit

A number of Henri Nouwen's own writings, his journals in particular, reflect his sensitive awareness of the relationship between spirit and place. For instance, key places such as Genesee or Daybreak, among others, have directly and profoundly contributed to the unique shape and texture of Nouwen's spiritual odyssey.

Along this same vein, Douglas Burton-Christie draws attention to recent works under the category of autobiographical reflection ("memoirs of place," as he prefers to call them) such as Kathleen Norris's best seller, *Dakota: A Spiritual Geography*. Norris's work and others like it focus upon a particular geography coupled with a specific person's experience—an apt reminder that place "cannot be conceived of in generic terms but must proceed from the description and narration of particular places"[5] involving communities of memories.

A Place of Belonging

This rich concept of place is especially illuminating. The idea of belonging—which Henri Nouwen identifies to be the very essence of community—does entail not only "our existence within networks of stable relationships," but also "a connection to specific places."[6] Such is, of course, universally true for all of us. As is often the case, we find ourselves gravitating toward certain communities that somehow provide us memorable links to our past, usually in the form of identifiable places and locations to which we can readily connect. We do congregate so naturally, so effortlessly, with "our people" who come from "our place."

At the same time, we feel like we actually belong to two simultaneous worlds—the ones we sometimes leave behind and the others we choose to embrace at certain junctures in our journey. It is thus helpful for us to recognize the inescapable paradox of human existence, which, according to writer Belden Lane, is, "an ever-renewed tension between exile and home."[7]

Living with Tension

Constantly in life, we all get pulled in either one of two directions: to stay put where we are or to launch on an uncharted territory. In his particular case, Henri Nouwen chose the latter at the onset of his career. He left his native Holland for the United States to explore opportunities wider than what his homeland could offer him.

Ironically, twenty-five years after, Nouwen still expressed some ambivalence about the decision he made: "On the one hand, I want to go my own way, and I am grateful for the freedom I have been given. On the other hand, I still desire to be acknowledged as a priest of Utrecht, informed about what's going on, and invited to make a contribution" (*SJ*:89). Of course, as we know it now, Nouwen's career move, in the end, proved to be a gain shared not only by America, but also the rest of the world.

Burton-Christie warns of the implicit dangers of giving in totally to either of the two impulses: stability or mobility. According to him, extreme impulses can result in "stagnation and fearfulness on one hand, rootlessness and loss of identity on the other."[8]

In analyzing Henri Nouwen's chosen life path, it is most likely that had Nouwen confined himself to Holland in the 1970s, he would have felt stifled by the religious constrictions governing that period and that could have led to his intellectual and spiritual stagnation. Removing himself from his familiar roots, however, did come with a price for Nouwen. While he tried to sustain his connections back home through the years, Nouwen remained the proverbial unwelcome prophet to his very own people—something about which Nouwen continually nursed some wounded feelings and never got over completely.[9]

Striving for Balance

We normally equate every inhabited space we call home as our "nest" or place of refuge. But, as Burton-Christie prompts us to see, "…[i]f a nest is a place of refuge, it is also a place from which to venture out into the world."[10]

Placement and Movement

This exact scenario depicted by Burton-Christie became real for Henri Nouwen. He used Yale and Harvard not so much as permanent nesting places but as his launching pads to access the larger world. It was while he was at Yale that Nouwen made short-term mission trips to Latin America, and it was also during his brief stint at Harvard that he traveled all over the United States, delivering lectures to draw the attention of Americans to the plight of the oppressed people in Latin America.

Even when Nouwen finally settled at L'Arche community, he still traveled to many places, often bringing along some of the community's handicapped members as he spoke and ministered to various audiences. As was the case at Harvard, Nouwen did not only bring L'Arche to the world, the world literally came to his doorsteps at L'Arche.[11]

Christianity itself, as accentuated by religious philosopher Michel de Certeau, is thought of as a "way of proceeding" and that the real essence of discipleship "simultaneously demands a particular 'placement' *and* a continual movement beyond each place in search of an 'elsewhere,' a 'further,' an ever greater."[12]

Location and Journeying

Somehow, the church, which always yearns to be stable, is likewise called to be a forward-moving community. As Nouwen himself understood it, each community possesses a certain stability that togetherness brings, but it also requires the mobility that displacement creates for the purpose of ministry (*RO*:153–55). As

Christ-followers, we must be willing to leave our comfort zones if our specific call for a given time requires that of us.

Thus the nature of the spiritual life unfolds unceasingly in a dialectic of location and journeying. Stability is crucial because we all long to be rooted. Yet mobility too is necessary and, moreover, freeing for some. It may very well represent "a lifesaving escape" as well as liberation from certain suffocating obligations.[13]

That seemed to be the scenario for Henri Nouwen insofar as Harvard was concerned. To a great extent, Nouwen's decision to abandon his prestigious post at Harvard was a matter of spiritual survival for him. To someone like Nouwen, who was unapologetically vocal about his faith, Harvard did not seem a conducive place. Personally, Nouwen deeply yearned for a breathing space to do what he really wanted to do: to speak about Jesus openly and without restraint.

Mobility can also present us with fresh challenges. The noble prospect of solidarity may push us beyond our familiar boundaries of social, cultural, and economic separations. We are summoned to find our relational identity beyond ourselves, and as Henri Nouwen envisioned it, even beyond our so-called togetherness. It was Nouwen's conscious identification with the marginalized members of society that led him to choose the tiny and obscure community of L'Arche over the towering reputation of an Ivy League school such as Harvard. Nouwen genuinely wanted "to belong to those who did not belong."[14]

A Necessary Synthesis

To balance stability and mobility, Burton-Christie proposes a synthesis that necessitates "a willingness to move motivated by the desire to make a commitment to place and community."[15] One has to be prepared to be uprooted, if necessary, and to actively seek to be rooted anew.

Henri Nouwen achieved this kind of synthesis. At long last in 1986, he burned all his bridges and responded to what he felt to be a vocational call from God to serve as pastor of Daybreak community. Having willingly uprooted himself from the world of academia, Nouwen strove to establish new roots at his newfound community with equal, if not greater, willingness and conscientiousness. All his efforts paid off. As destiny would have it for him, L'Arche ultimately proved to be *the* place to be for the final decade of Henri Nouwen's life.

While he continued to travel occasionally to speak outside his community, Nouwen remained faithful to his expressed commitments to his flock at Daybreak, always eager to return to their loving embrace. At L'Arche, Henri Nouwen discovered his temporary earthly home before resting in his permanent heavenly home.

The Local and Universal God

In order to hold together the tension between stability and mobility, one must also bring to bear the mysterious character of God, who is both local and universal, immanent as well as transcendent. Robert Hamma directs us to the practical realization that

> [a] universal awareness of God's presence forces us to look for God in the places where we may be fearful to go—places of poverty, places of violence, places of illness. And an awareness of God in a particular place calls us to look deeply and contemplatively at the places that reveal God to us.[16]

This kind of universal awareness of God was what drove Henri Nouwen out of himself into the uncomfortable frontiers of Latin America, thus intensifying his restlessness. It was, however, Nouwen's more personal and particular awareness of God that put him in a relatively settled place of decreasing—though not disappearing—restlessness.

Such particularity pointed directly to his life-changing experience with Adam at L'Arche, the severely handicapped young man who was assigned under Nouwen's personal care. Nouwen declared in retrospect: "L'Arche became my community and Daybreak my home because of Adam....[He] gave me a sense of belonging. He rooted me in the truth of my physical being, anchored me in my community, and gave me a deep experience of God's presence in our life together" (*A*:126). Indeed, God can choose to reveal himself and make his presence felt in both the universal and particular settings in our life.

At Home while on the Way

Finally, within the broader context of ministry and service, author Eugene Peterson poses a needful challenge for us to yoke the polarities of what he refers to as *geography* and *eschatology*—the conceptual equivalent of the "here-and-now" and the "here-after." Indeed, it is imperative that we learn to embrace the locale and immerse ourselves in the particulars of ministry. But never must we lose sight of the eternal.

We are called to be presently involved yet forward looking, future oriented, and not stuck. As Peterson urges us, we have to imbibe in both "the sense of everyday ordinary place and the sense of shaping eternal purpose."[17] This calls for the creative act of continually envisioning ourselves—to use Henri Nouwen's expression—as being "at home while still on the way." On the whole, this particular version of the "now-and-the-not-yet" admittedly triggers tension and an ever increasing sense of restlessness in all of us. It certainly did for Nouwen.

A Long, Restless Journey of Preparation

So what do we make of Henri Nouwen's restless seeking? Nouwen first imagined the Trappist monastery might be the place of solace for his wandering soul. Then the prospect of settling for a life of service among the poor of Peru became a real desire to end his frenetic existence. As we now know it, neither came about for Nouwen. Daybreak ended up being the home for which Nouwen was desperate.

Was L'Arche a convenient cop-out for Henri Nouwen? Had his restlessness of heart become uncontainable? Did the opening at L'Arche provide him both an interior and exterior shield for a bruised self-esteem and a tarnished reputation about to fall apart as a consequence of his "failed" mission in Latin America? Or was L'Arche the gracious and timely provision of a loving God to a restless soul? Perhaps it was some combination of the above; one can only conjecture. One thing we do know for certain:

The L'Arche experience transformed Henri completely. Henri was someone who needed a lot of love, and at Daybreak he experienced some of the love he needed. Although it was a loving community, Henri also found Daybreak to be a disarming, unsettling place. His lifestyle and assumptions were fundamentally challenged. A man of words, he suddenly found himself among people who could not understand words. A man of action, he suddenly found himself among people who could not move their bodies. He was profoundly affected by the vulnerability of those around him.[18]

The truth is that the restless struggle to follow God became for Nouwen "a long journey of preparation—of preparing oneself to truly die for others" as well as to self (*BM:65–66*). Needless to say, it was also a slow, painful process all the way—one we are all bound to undergo.

The Home Nouwen Longed For

In his book *The Longing for Home*, author Frederick Buechner allows us to see the deeper meaning of home from two vantage points: "...the one we remember and the one we dream, not only where we're from but where we're going." Unpacking Buechner's insight further, there seems to be a significant weight to the saying that "the places we know and love, and the people who inhabit them, offer a glimpse of the spiritual home we anticipate."[19]

For one, Henri Nouwen's actual experience appears to substantiate the veracity of such saying. L'Arche, which became Nouwen's earthly home during the last decade of his life, approximated for him everything he longed to experience to the fullest in his future heavenly home: a community marked by unity in diversity and populated by people with vast differences—cultural, religious, political, socioeconomic, educational—yet enjoying overwhelming love and acceptance from one another.

Fellowship of the Weak

Most significantly, L'Arche became for Nouwen the concrete embodiment of the convictions that captured his life, foremost of which was to be in solidarity with the weak. Far from situating itself as a community of power, L'Arche typified a fellowship of the weak. Nouwen was eager to immerse himself totally in the life of this peculiar kind of community. L'Arche fulfilled Nouwen's yearning to experience genuine belonging with people to whom society, by and large, fails to extend a warm sense of belonging.

Fraternal Identification

There was no doubt that the community of L'Arche was Nouwen's newfound home. Since "home is as much an idea as it is the physical spaces into which we knit our daily lives," it follows in a way that "*where* we are makes us *who* we are."[20] Such became true for Henri Nouwen in that it was at L'Arche where he was able to face his own handicaps squarely and identify with and be fully embraced by its handicapped members as one of them.

Surrounded by a supportive and caring community of the weak and powerless, Henri Nouwen felt the freedom to abandon himself to this group of wounded yet gifted creatures like him. To this community, Nouwen did not seem to have trouble throwing all his energy, even coming close to the edge of losing himself in his intense desire to identify with its members' plight and destiny.

Henri Nouwen's consuming drive toward solidarity unraveled the "fraternal" essence of his self-concept. In a decisive way, Nouwen identified his own journey with his chosen community, seeing in its embodiment an intimate connection with his personal struggles and aspirations. Authors Donald and Walter Capps explain that for someone who has this fraternal dispositional factor, "the basic impetus behind his words and actions is not projection, but the recognition of his formative place in the destiny of his people."[21]

Clearly, this was something that played itself out within the context of Nouwen's life situation at L'Arche. Beyond that, however, Nouwen genuinely wanted to identify with the descending way of Jesus as a way to enter more authentically into the gospel story.[22]

Much as L'Arche paved the way for a more centered and less conflicted Nouwen, the struggles of his everyday life remained unabated. Restlessness continued to plague him.

An Inconsolable Longing

The lifelong battle to secure peace and quiet for his soul never subsided for Henri Nouwen. It was never meant to; for "inside each of us, at the center of our lives, there is a tension, an ache, an insatiable fire that cannot be quieted."[23] C. S. Lewis calls it the "inconsolable longing" from which all of us suffer. It is a piercing reminder of the reality of imperfection on this side of heaven. Lewis offers a plausible reason for its stubborn presence in you and me: "If I find in myself a desire which no experience in this world can satisfy, the most probable explanation is that I was made for another world."[24]

Although Henri Nouwen could not fully resolve his own restlessness, he realized that it always brought him back to God, the Perfect One whom he was ultimately seeking. Thus it could be remarked that, in the midst of imperfection, Nouwen was, at least, drawing closer to Perfection.

A Wounded Healer

Restlessness goes with a dreaded sense of incompleteness. One author described Henri Nouwen—and for that matter, all of us—straightforwardly: "Henri was complex and unfinished"; but unlike many of us, "he knew it well and did not pretend otherwise."[25]

None of us is whole, at least not yet. We are a damaged, broken, and wounded lot. Not only did Henri Nouwen acknowledge this intrinsic condition we share with all of humanity; he vividly lived it. One of Nouwen's biographers commented that he has been portrayed by some people as a "saint with wounds."[26] At best he has been identified with a memorable phrase that has become the virtual cornerstone of his spirituality, "the wounded healer"—a concept that was not actually his original concoction, although, without a doubt, Nouwen built quite a reputation on it.

One of Henri Nouwen's friends was able to put his finger on a deep-seated desire Nouwen had repressed for years, which only resurfaced in Nouwen's consciousness while he was taking his sabbatical year. "It has to do with [Nouwen's] search for community and [his] deep yearning for completeness," his friend Jim pointed out (*SJ*:122).

What triggered this yearning for Nouwen was his initial exposure and later his friendship with the South African trapeze artists known as the Flying Rodleighs. He was enthralled while watching them perform in Freiburg, Germany, in 1991. Through their trapeze act, Nouwen envisioned a rich metaphor for the spiritual life. For instance, he saw the idea of complete surrender and trust exemplified in the cooperative act between the flier and the catcher.[27] Nouwen even seriously considered writing a book about the circus troupe but hesitated many times about pushing through with the project. Reflecting upon the group's initial impact on him stirred up all kinds of inner sensations inside of him, leaving him in strange awe.

> When I first saw the Rodleighs, something very deep and intimate within me was touched....[S]eeing the Rodleighs catapulted me into a new consciousness. There in the air I saw the artistic realization of my deepest yearnings. It was so intense that even today I do not dare to write about it because it requires a radical new step not only in my writing but also in my life. (*SJ*: 121–22)

Just what was underneath all that heartfelt recollection of his? To be sure, Henri Nouwen's transparent revelation of his inner thoughts revealed that this particular episode in his life involving the Rodleighs was more than a passing fancy, or simply a peripheral note to his eventful existence.

Perhaps his friend Jim was right: "...friendship, family, cooperation, artistic expression, love, commitment, and much more. It all has to do with community" (*SJ*:122). This could well be what the Rodleighs meant to Nouwen; but there could also be something deeper than meets the eye.

It seemed that for Henri Nouwen, underlying all that longing for community that Jim pinpointed was a profound feeling of "aloneness." What is reckoned to be a universal feeling appears to be a far more pronounced reality in Nouwen's experience—so painful it could be likened to an existential wound: the inner wound of loneliness.

Wound of Loneliness

Few artists have impacted Henri Nouwen as much as his fellow Dutchman Vincent van Gogh. He referred to his affinity with the famous painter with a tender feeling of soul connection: "This deeply wounded and immensely gifted Dutchman brought me in touch with my own brokenness...in ways nobody else could."[28] Interestingly, when Nouwen died, his casket was strewn with bright sunflowers—a familiar motif in Van Gogh's paintings—which formed an intriguing but fitting contrast to the dark cloud of loneliness both Nouwen and Van Gogh experienced in life.

What was this inner wound that Henri Nouwen seemed to be born with? Nouwen himself characterized it with such deep, personal familiarity—"this immense need for affection, and this immense fear of rejection"—while pointing to its fragility in his own life (*SJ*:25). Painfully, he recalled at one time—upon reading the poetry Michaelangelo had composed for a young Roman nobleman named Tommaso Cavalieri, describing their affectionate relationship—how the poetic words he was reading seemed to leap off the pages and "evoke deep feelings in [him]," exposing his heart to his "true dependence on human affection and love" (*SJ*:131–32). With such bared heart, Nouwen expressed this perennial sentiment in one of his prayers to Jesus: "I continue to look for affection, support, acceptance and praise among my fellow human beings, always expecting from them what only you can give" (*HSH*:20).

The reality of loneliness for Henri Nouwen was compounded by the fact that he was a priest who faithfully committed himself to the vow of celibacy. The very prospect of a real-life companion of any kind was therefore totally out of the question for him. Writing a letter of consolation to his father six months after the death of his mother in 1978, Nouwen reminded his father: "...you have a son who has been alone since he left your house. Becoming a priest for me has in fact meant to enter the road of 'the long loneliness,' as Dorothy Day called it, and my many physical and spiritual journeys have deepened that experience even further."[29] Despite his aching wish for his "inner darkness" to leave him, Nouwen had to learn to face the reality that his sorrow-filled existence was always there to haunt him like a ghost in the dark. In one of his last books, Nouwen expressed his repeated lament:

> The...struggle to find someone to love me is still there; unfulfilled needs for affirmation...remain alive in me....I experience deep sorrow that I have not become who I wanted to be, and that the God to whom I have prayed so much has not given me what I have most desired. (*CYD*:33–34)

Mixed in with the inner murmuring going on inside Nouwen's heart, however, was a shining sliver of hope:

> I know that the longer I live, the more suffering I will see and that the more suffering I see, the more sorrow I will be asked to live. But it is this deep human sorrow that unites my wounded heart with the heart of humanity. It is in this mystery of union in suffering that hope is hidden. (*WJ*:29)

Henri Nouwen, of all people, knew from experience that loneliness is "one of the most universal sources of human suffering..." (*RO*:25). In the words of author Ronald Rolheiser, "To be human is to be lonely," but he hastens to add, "[T]o be human, however, is also to respond."[30]

How did Henri Nouwen choose to respond to the excruciating wound of loneliness in his life? He faced it squarely and befriended it; but most of all, he chose to channel it to ministry with other wounded souls. Nouwen's life encourages us all to do the same by refusing to hide or be afraid of the raw material of our lives. He said:

> When each of us can hold firm to our own cup, with its many sorrows and joys, claiming it as our unique life, then we too can lift it up for others to see and encourage them to lift up their lives as well....[T]he wounds of our individual lives, which seem intolerable when lived alone, become sources of healing when we live them as part of a fellowship of mutual care. (*CYD*:57)

Henri Nouwen modeled to all the kind of painful transparency that we rarely find among ministers of the Gospel and caregivers. It is no secret that Nouwen was a heavily conflicted man who battled depression and even suffered a complete nervous breakdown. For the greater part, his lonely life was one tormenting existence.

Wounded Servant-Minister

Loneliness, however, did not prevent Henri Nouwen from ministering to others: "He guided many through the dark places of doubt and loss of faith. While he was doing this for others he was himself powerfully afflicted by dark thoughts and mental pains. He knew anxiety and depression, from which there was only temporary release."[31]

Nouwen took comfort in the knowledge that just as "Jesus' wounds remain visible in his risen body...our wounds are not taken away, but become sources of hope to others" (*RD*:163). If one is to truly care for others' well-being, Nouwen believes, "one must offer one's own vulnerable self to others as a source of healing."[32] For Nouwen, the crucial question is not "'How can we hide our wounds?' so we don't have to be embarrassed but 'How can we put our woundedness in *the service of others* [emphasis mine]?' When our wounds cease to be a source of shame and become a source of healing, we have become wounded healers" (*BJ*:July 8).

Only the bruised, wounded minister can powerfully connect with those who are badly wounded. A true wounded healer, according to Henri Nouwen, serves by "listen[ing] to a person in pain without having to speak about his or her wounds" (*BJ*:July 10). Real healing happens when each of us learns to listen to our wounds with attentiveness and love. Ministry is not about finding ways to get rid of people's pain, but about enabling others to welcome and embrace it. For healing to take place, pain needs to be confronted for what it really is.

Henri Nouwen learned from firsthand experience of pain in his own life that "[t]he first step to healing is not a step away from the pain but a step toward it" (*LOB*:75). The real challenge for each of us is to keep "living [our] wounds through instead of thinking them through"—that is, "to let [our] wounds go down into [our] heart" (*IVL*:109). To avoid the extremes of either becoming too engrossed with our pain or staying as far away from the very wound we seek to heal, Nouwen urges us to "work around [our] abyss" (*IVL*:109).

We know only too well that people have ways of deadening themselves so as to avoid the experience of further pain in life. Henri Nouwen understood clearly what contemporary therapists are realizing more—that the dirty job of a real counselor is to radically remove the client's chosen painkillers, metaphorically speaking.

Henri Nouwen's enduring concept and portrayal of the wounded healer did not lack its share of critics though. One in particular complained: "Many see the Nouwen minister as a weakling....The wounded-healer pastor may become an inward-looking chaplain of the emotions who forgets his [*sic*] function as a prophet of God and servant of those in need."[33] However, Henri Nouwen, in his celebrated book *The Wounded Healer*, warned against a form of "spiritual exhibitionism" that grossly misuses the wounded healer concept. From his point of view, "open wounds stink and do not heal" (*WH*:88). Nouwen was in no way promoting the morbid idea of wallowing in our woundedness. On the contrary, he wanted to encourage us to "find the freedom to step over our wounds" (*HN*:45). Elsewhere, Nouwen talked about the importance of "tending our wounds first," for he truly believed that "[a]s long as our wounds are open and bleeding, we scare others away. But after someone has tended to our wounds, they no longer frighten us or others" (*BJ*:July 9).

In reality, a Christ full of power emerges brilliantly through Henri Nouwen's wounded state. Like Paul, though Nouwen was weak, he was strong because of Christ's power evident in and through him. His own woundedness served as a vast channel through which God's limitless power could freely be displayed. "It is indeed through our broken, vulnerable, mortal ways of being that the healing power of the eternal God becomes visible to us," Nouwen claimed (*CFM*:144). In Paul's words: "But we have this treasure in clay jars, so that it may be made clear that this extraordinary power belongs to God and does not come from us" (2 Cor 4:7).

Both during Henri Nouwen's life and after his death, his ministry was amply blessed. He did not have to do anything; he simply lived out his humanity and his unique calling. The core of his humanity was his being "wounded" and the core of his true calling was his being a "healer."[34] Henri Nouwen lived both core truths well.

In restlessness as in woundedness, Henri Nouwen embodied imperfection. In both, struggle became the common thread of his experience. As a genuine seeker, Nouwen was restless. As a true healer, he was deeply wounded. As a real struggler, Henri Nouwen was faithful. Struggle as the stuff of imperfection for Nouwen (and us too) is the final theme to which we turn our attention next.

A Faithful Struggler

At the heart of an authentic spiritual life lies the experience of struggle. As Henri Nouwen paints it, our new life is "a life of joy, but also of sacrifice. It is a glorious life, but also one of suffering. It is a life of peace, but also of struggle" (HSH:43–44). Our entire spiritual journey constitutes struggle.

Struggle is a central feature in the writings of Henri Nouwen. Nouwen must have truly believed with the ancient Orthodox monks that in the spiritual life, "[w]e advance as we learn how to fall and rise, and still keep going."[35] On this front, Henri Nouwen felt no shame to share his own personal battles with the entire world. From experience he testified again and again that struggle was the stuff of imperfection he had to learn to live with. In Nouwen, as in all of us, virtues and imperfections reside together. As Carolyn Whitney-Brown phrases it: "the gift and struggle of his life remained intertwined."[36]

I venture to say that Henri Nouwen's struggle is itself a gift. For one thing, it is the open acknowledgment of his own failings and struggles that gives people "permission to search their own hearts more honestly and more deeply."[37] Many find themselves readily connecting with Nouwen because he was able to give voice to their own, often unspoken, experiences. In Marci Whitney-Schenck's way of putting it, Henri Nouwen "could communicate the human experience in such a way that readers found themselves cloaked in Christ's love. He could express people's yearning for God, and although he didn't always have the answers to spiritual vacuousness, he could articulate a vulnerability that people embraced."[38]

"My books," Nouwen noted without any qualms, "aren't particularly from someone who has his act together. They are from someone always searching, wondering. I trust my struggle is not just for me. It is given to me for others too."[39] Exactly what is the essence of this struggle to which Henri Nouwen refers and in which we all participate as believers in the spiritual journey?

Nature of Struggle

First of all, the struggle consists of our active engagement with a battle that rages unceasingly both internally and externally. The specific sources of conflict about which the Bible speaks include the world, the devil, and indwelling sin, which works through our "flesh" (see, e.g., 1 John 2:15–17; Eph 6:12; Rom 7:14–24). The fiercest struggle, it seems, is the internal battle we wage in our "flesh"—one that Paul vividly portrays in Romans 7.[40]

For the most part, Henri Nouwen focused on this inner struggle. The intensity of the struggle pictured in Romans 7 generates an intriguing merit when set against the equally compelling reality of victory promised in Romans 8.

On one hand, Romans 7 exposes us to the realistic though not necessarily the ideal side of the spiritual life—that of ongoing struggle to maintain the reality of our freedom in Christ in our daily experience. On the other hand, Romans 8 presents to us what seems to many to be an idealistic but very real side of the spiritual life: a life of significant victory via the enabling power of the Holy Spirit who gives us a foretaste of spiritual freedom in the present age.

An integrated treatment of Romans 7 and 8 lets us see these two realities coexisting like two sides of the same coin. As biblical scholar C. E. B. Cranfield urges us, we need to "resolutely hold chapters 7 and 8 together, in spite of the obvious tension between them, and see in them not two successive stages but two different aspects, two contemporaneous realities, of the Christian life."[41]

The victory spoken about in Romans 8 is more meaningfully experienced from and within the context of struggle depicted in

Romans 7. One can have struggle without victory but no one can ever have real victory without real struggle. As Henri Nouwen himself recognizes, "Spiritual freedom requires a fierce spiritual battle" (*IVL*:xix). Victory is best viewed within the context of a real battle. Nouwen attests: "The battle is real....[y]ou will only know what victory is when you have been part of the battle" (*GD*:71–72).

The very tension that exists between Romans 7 and 8 is enough to set in motion the experience of struggle for the believer. In a practical sense, Merton has a valid point in describing the spiritual life as "a kind of dialectic between ideals and reality," although he readily qualifies that it is "a dialectic, not a compromise."[42]

For some though, the experience of spiritual life more resembles that of a spiritual tug-of-war. Henri Nouwen himself was no stranger to that kind of an experience wherein he was constantly being pulled in different directions. His personal journals can sometimes read more like a dizzying record of contradictory statements than a coherent expression of thoughts and feelings. They showcase, more than anything, Nouwen's continual struggles to translate his intentions into actions, his ideas into reality, and his endless professions into concrete expressions. Nouwen himself conceded: "There are so many contradictions within me....the distance between insight and practice is huge" (*SJ*:13). As if to clinch his litany of confessions, Nouwen, in a journal entry he wrote one Easter Sunday, made this honest admission to himself: "[M]y faith and unbelief are never far from each other" (*SJ*:143). Sue Mosteller concluded that Nouwen's "struggle to close the gap between the ideal and the reality is so real, so painful, and so human!"[43]

Added to Nouwen's already complicated struggle were common contradictory impulses arising from within him. An example is recorded in his Genesee diary: "When I receive many letters I complain that I am too busy, and when I receive none I complain about lack of attention; when I work a lot I complain about lack of time to study and pray, when I work little I feel guilty for not making a contribution (*GD*:202)."

Nowhere was this conflicted side of Nouwen magnified more clearly than in his personal struggle with friendship relationships.

His struggle usually stemmed from his overwhelming desire to find "a way to satisfy [his] deep yearning for intimacy and affection" (*GD*:170). Nouwen recognized that his greatest pain was always tied in with his relationships with the people closest to him—those whom he loved and who loved him.[44]

In his mind, Henri Nouwen was likewise fully aware that "[t]he stronger our expectation that another human being will fulfill our deepest desires, the greater the pain is when we are confronted with the limitations of human relationships" (*HN*:125). At the same time, Nouwen, like many of us, often found it extremely difficult to apply to his own situation the truths that he grasped in his head but sometimes got blocked in his heart—especially when he allowed his neediness to get the better of him.

A classic example was his fluctuating estimation of his relationship with both Nathan Ball and Sue Mosteller. With mixed feelings, Nouwen expressed this about them: "The moments of ecstasy and agony connected with both of them mark my nine years at Daybreak....I have felt rejected as well as supported, abandoned as well as embraced, hated as well as loved" (*SJ*:7).

Henri Nouwen's intimate diaries reveal the story of a quiet struggler who wrestled with tortuous feelings of anxiety, deep-seated insecurity, hurt, rejection, persistent anger, resentment, hatred, jealousy, passive-aggressive attitudes, and a multitude of doubts—all closely related to his wide web of complex relationships. None of these struggles is unfamiliar to any of our own experiences except that, unlike most of us, Nouwen has freely gone on record to talk about them openly. Yet like many of us, he genuinely longed to overcome this lifelong battle. At the same time, Nouwen acknowledged the existence of spiritual tension that made the process of overcoming every conceivable struggle a challenge of great proportion.

Presence of Tension

For one who is still very much a part of this present world trying to live as though already belonging to the age to come, a real tension exists.[45] To begin with, "the believer has not yet arrived, is not yet perfect, is always *in via*," and as such, is bound to experience "the tension between a work 'begun' but not yet 'complete,' between fulfillment and consummation, between a decisive 'already' and still to be worked out 'not yet.'"[46]

David Wenham could not agree more that "[i]t is indeed by living the life of the new age in the old age that [the believer] becomes conformed to Christ's likeness."[47] This reassuring thought, Henri Nouwen pointed out, can motivate one to deal patiently with the struggle of having "to live for a while with the 'not yet'"…knowing full well that one's "deepest, truest self is not yet home" (*IVL*:50).

Henri Nouwen posed a revealing question to which he volunteered his own answer: "Can the tension be resolved in an integrated life?…[F]ew have accomplished this wholeness. I certainly have not" (*SJ*:39). One other question begs to be answered: Just how does one really deal with spiritual tension? What seems to be Henri Nouwen's "secret"—not only in terms of managing spiritual tension, but even more importantly, of keeping himself integrated and in one solid piece against all the forces threatening to make him crumble as a person.

It may not be all that profitable to psychoanalyze Henri Nouwen in an attempt to explain his complexity as a human being. We already know his negative propensities, including his obsessions and insecurities. The more puzzling question is: How did he live with all those so-called negatives and still exert the most positive impact on others? How else does one explain how the insecure Nouwen could project such confidence, or that the scattered brain and often distracted Nouwen could also be such a focused and centered person?[48]

Behind Henri Nouwen's seemingly split persona lay a dogged and unique capacity to integrate. His natural skill to integrate was precisely what enabled him to manage an otherwise tension-filled existence. Nouwen's mind seemed automatically conditioned to operate not in an either/or but in a both/and modality. Nouwen was able to allow two seeming opposites to be brought together in order to strike a more unified scheme that consequently would lessen (not exactly eliminate) the presence of tension.

This innate pull to integrate and blur polarities was what kept Nouwen's sanity intact. Instead of being torn apart into pieces each time he was faced with a whole array of contradictions (real or imagined), Nouwen was able to regulate the tension by responding accordingly.[49]

Learning to manage tension in this way, amazing as it appears, does not resolve tension altogether. The presence of tension functions as a grim reminder that the struggle of life also incorporates the inevitable presence of darkness looming both inside and outside all of us.

Presence of Darkness

The stark reality of darkness took the forms of personal and spiritual struggle for Henri Nouwen. Inwardly he battled with his private "demons," so to speak. Sexual guilt, shame, anxiety, and insecurity cumulatively represented for Nouwen an ominous presence of internal darkness that weighed him down severely. Much as he wanted to dispel it, darkness hovered about like a heavy cloud in his life that simply would not move away. Even when it seemed like he had finally found the "light" at L'Arche after a long, dark journeying experience, Henri Nouwen still admitted:

> Life in community does not keep the darkness away. To the contrary. It seems that the light that attracted me to L'Arche also made me conscious of the darkness in myself. Jealousy, anger, the feeling of being rejected or neglected, the sense of not truly belonging—all of these emerged in the context of a community....Community life has opened me up to the real spiritual combat: the struggle to keep moving toward the light precisely when the darkness is so real. (*RPS*:136)

Despite his awareness that times of darkness and doubt are standard ingredients for a life of faith," Nouwen never envisioned going through the worst of them.

It was while serving as pastor of L'Arche community that Henri Nouwen encountered the darkest episode of his life. It concerned the breakdown of his friendship with Nathan Ball, something already alluded to earlier in chapter one. In his anguished account, we encounter Nouwen's version of the "dark night" in his own words:

Here I was,...flat on the ground and in total darkness. What had happened? I had come face to face with my nothing-ness. It was as if all that had given my life meaning was pulled away and I could see nothing in front of me but a bottomless abyss....I felt that God had abandoned me. It was as if the house I had finally found had no floors. The anguish completely paralyzed me....All had become dark-ness. (*IVL*:xiii–xiv)

The "dark night of the soul," a phrase most identified with the sixteenth-century mystic and poet St. John of the Cross, has become a familiar part of our contemporary vocabulary. Over the years it has been used as a catch phrase to refer to anything but good that happens in every person's life.

It is true that even for Christians there always exists the pos-sibility that their relationship with God can be "shaken, lessened, or interrupted for various reasons:...[including] God's with-drawing the sense of his presence and allowing them to walk in darkness."[50] Many of us, at some point in our Christian experi-ence, can identify feeling a sense of spiritual desertion or aban-donment that the Psalmist talked about (see e.g., Ps 30:7) and that Henri Nouwen himself did go through. Everybody passes through some dark period in one's spiritual journey. Sometimes, the darkness can be so thick that one wonders whether anything can actually pierce through it or push it back. Calling the phe-nomenon "dark" almost automatically leaves a negative impres-sion in the minds of many.

In reality, as psychiatrist-turned-spiritual-director Gerald May insists, "The dark night is a profoundly good thing....in which we are liberated from attachments and compulsions and empowered to live and love more freely." "[D]eepening love," May explains, "is the real purpose of the dark night of the soul....[It] helps us become who we are created to be: lovers of God and one another."[51]

Henri Nouwen came out of his encounter with the dark night of his own soul with a far greater motivation to love more deeply. Because Nouwen decided "to choose, in the face of it all, not death but life," he was able "to look back at that period of [his] life and see it as a time of intense purification that had led [him] gradually to a new inner freedom, a new hope, and a new creativity" (*IVL*: xvii–xviii; 59–60).

Thus it becomes evident, as demonstrated by Henri Nouwen's experience, that the struggle involved in any kind of dark night passage is by no means a sign of death. Constance Fitzgerald illuminates this truth further: "Dark night is instead a sign of life, of growth, of development in our relationship with God, in our best human relationships, and in our societal life. It is a sign to move on in hope to a new vision, a new experience."[52]

Indeed, we continue to grow as we continue to learn. The dark night struggle itself is a momentous learning experience. Strange as it may appear, it is an occasion to learn through the presence of darkness. As author Wendy Wright poetically renders it: "How dark the seeing. How fragmentary. Mostly it consists of learning to free fall. Learning to trust the constant somersaulting. Learning to live with spiritual vertigo. Learning to love darkness. Learning to trust the brief glimpses. Learning that blindness is its own seeing."[53]

Henri Nouwen openly embraced the reality of struggle as a normative experience of spiritual imperfection. He welcomed spiritual tension and learned to manage its imposing presence. He accepted spiritual darkness and willingly passed through its black corridors without losing his spiritual vision. Through it all, Henri Nouwen never gave up on the struggle but remained faithful.

Faithfulness amidst Struggle

Faithfulness is the one outstanding trait for which Henri Nouwen is best remembered by people closest to him. In Nathan Ball's recollection, "So often and in so many ways, Henri expressed his desire to be faithful—faithful to God, to his own inner self, to the demands of love, to friendships, and to his chosen vocation as a priest."[54] Living with God demands faithfulness. It is a serious call which, Nouwen insisted, "must be lived in the choices of every moment" (*IVL*:23). Without question, such a call involves faithfulness even in the thick of struggle.

Henri Nouwen heeded this call in the midst of his ongoing struggle with human relationships. In his heart he resolved that "whatever [he] will 'feel,' it is important that [he] keep[s] making inner choices of faithfulness" (*SJ*:7). To him, determination was key in the exercise of faithfulness.

Drawing upon this same attitude of determination, Nouwen confronted head-on what many assumed to be the crux of his struggle, which was dealing with his homosexual orientation. Michael Ford's revealing portrait of Henri Nouwen exposed this largely hidden struggle of Nouwen and depicted the priest's sexuality as "a source of deep anxiety and conflict" due to his unbending "commitment to live out his vow of celibacy."[55]

Nouwen's view of celibacy went beyond the common idea of staying in an unmarried state. Celibacy, to him, was more of "a lifestyle in which we try to witness to the priority of God in all relationships" (*CR*:50). As implied, to be celibate meant to consciously disallow anything that could usurp God's rightful place in our hearts.

Celibacy was no small issue for Nouwen, who understood well the complications of trying to live a chaste life (*RD*:169). Still, Nouwen faithfully committed to conduct his "hidden and secret life" with purity of heart no matter what (*SJ*:24). For someone whose craving for human love and affection seemed insatiable, the protracted struggle involved could only be brutally painful.

To the best of his closest friends' knowledge, "Nouwen may have struggled, but he made no compromises with his convictions."[56] Even when presented by well-meaning homosexual friends with several options for dealing with his sexual life, Nouwen dismissed each of them and decided—again and again—to keep living, however torturously, with his inner wound.[57]

"Guided by the deep awareness that we are called to be living signs of God's faithful presence among us...." (*HN*:129), Henri Nouwen quietly struggled his way through until the end of his life. This he did without disintegrating because God faithfully sustained him all the way.

A Spiritual Profile of an Imperfect Saint

Many of us know Henri Nouwen via his prolific writings. Writing was just about the only steady thing in his frenzied lifestyle. The very act of writing became for him a source of therapeutic survival during the darkest period of his life (*IVL*:xvi).

We can safely paint a portrait of Henri Nouwen—from several different angles to be sure, even if it is a general one—because he has chosen to reveal himself candidly in all of his writings. By his doing so, Nouwen also allowed us to see ourselves through his life. His pen was perhaps his sharpest instrument to cut incisively through our hearts. Today he still continues to reach into the deepest parts of many by "holding up...his own lived experience as a reflecting glass, as it were, into which we can gaze and probe deeper dimensions of who we are, a mirror into which we can look and discover ourselves anew, both in our vulnerabilities, but also in our hidden potential, our true destinies."[58]

Still, the element of imperfection in Nouwen comes to full view when, sooner or later, one realizes that "a certain disconnection between [Nouwen's] writing and his living" existed and that Nouwen "always managed to write way beyond what he himself could actually live."[59] A former member of L'Arche articulated this reality so well:

> When I think of Henri, I think of two "books": one is the book that Henri wrote 40 times, yet couldn't quite live; the other is the book that Henri lived for almost 65 years, yet couldn't quite write. The second book waits to be written, as the meaning of Henri's life and wisdom reveal themselves now, after his death.[60]

No more accurate sketch of Nouwen's life is needed other than what has already been graphically portrayed by the person himself. It is a spirituality of imperfection that is no less deep, no less authentic. As to whether Nouwen's imperfection is ultimately a repelling reality or an enigmatic source of blessing, many will contend the latter because they, like myself, continue to be grateful recipients of it. Henri Nouwen's profound impact upon thousands of lives whom he had never even encountered personally is surely beyond telling.

While Henri Nouwen wrote extensively about himself, it was never to make himself out to be the point. For the most part, he shared his struggles clearly with the benefit of others in view.

Nouwen did not want his imperfections to serve as a convenient excuse not to reach out to others. Ministering to people always seemed his highest priority. Henri Nouwen was of the conviction that even "while we ourselves are overwhelmed by our own weaknesses and limitations, we can still be so transparent that the Spirit of God, the divine counselor, can shine through us and bring light to others" (*LR*:68). In many ways, it was his struggle and imperfection that qualified him even more to serve and to minister to others.

In his book *The Holy Longing*, Ronald Rolheiser wrote a moving dedication to Henri Nouwen that best captures Nouwen's "imperfect" influence upon so many:

> By sharing his own struggles, he mentored us all, helping us to pray while not knowing how to pray, to rest while feeling restless, to be at peace while tempted, to feel safe while still anxious, to be surrounded by a cloud of light while still in darkness, and to love while still in doubt.[61]

How can such an imperfect vessel also be a fountain out of which abundant blessings flow? What accounted for much of the impact of Henri Nouwen's spirituality?

Despite what may sound like a platitudinous rhetoric, I daresay, it was Jesus, Nouwen's Jesus, that made all the difference in his spirituality: "Nouwen embraced his crosses, carried them, and allowed them to lead him to Jesus."[62] Much as many would have preferred Henri Nouwen's woundedness feature less prominently in his life, Robert Jonas, his close friend and confidante, cleverly reminds us that "his ever-present, accompanying shadow was there only because of the Light in which he walked."[63] Henri Nouwen did walk with Jesus, his true love and the true lover of his wounded soul. Passionately and unashamedly he declared:

> Jesus has to be and to become ever more the center of my life. It is not enough that Jesus is my teacher, my guide, my source of inspiration. It is not even enough that he is my companion on the journey, my friend and my brother. Jesus must become the heart of my heart, the fire of my life, the love of my soul,

the bridegroom of my spirit. He must become my only thought, my only concern, my only desire.[64]

Two voices constantly vied for Nouwen's attention: "One encouraged him to succeed and achieve, while the other called him to simply rest in the comfort that he was 'the beloved' of God." Finally he heeded the second voice during the last decade of his life.[65]

On September 21, 1996, the restless, wounded, and struggling soul of God's beloved at long last found peace, wholeness, and contentment in the arms of his Eternal Lover in God's eternal home. The world mourned the death of a saint so scarred, so wounded, so imperfect that the church to which he belonged might consider him the least likely candidate for beatification, much less, canonization. The Christian world, however, lost a real saint who by his life demonstrated that the journey to perfection is through imperfection.

Conclusion

Today the phenomenon of spirituality attracts people who are stimulated far less by the will to understand than by the will to experience something and anything. Under this circumstance, it is refreshing to have a reliable guide such as Henri Nouwen who can steer us in the right direction and provide a perspective consistent with the message of the Gospel.

Without claiming to have the last word, Nouwen offers, via his provocative writings, an expansive view of spirituality that is at once unified, holistic, and integrative. Far from merely coating his teaching about spirituality with a thin veneer of scriptural-sounding truth, Henri Nouwen articulates a message centered on biblical love—which lies at the heart of authentic Christian spirituality.

Through the example of his own life, Henri Nouwen demonstrates how spirituality essentially coinheres with psychology, ministry, and theology in a way that parallels and supports the main thrust of the Great Commandment. From his vantage point, the spiritual life consists of three intersecting movements directed to self, to others, and to God, all within the overall context of a journey of love: love of self, love of others, and love of God.

By claiming that psychology coinheres with spirituality, the soul and the spirit are assumed to commingle in the experience of every person who functions as a psychospiritual being. Moreover, the coinherence between the two indicates that the knowledge of self and the knowledge of God are inextricably bound together. Spirituality within a holistic framework is lived at the nexus of becoming more fully human and more fully divine. The joint pursuit of wholeness and holiness essentially defines the integrated thrust of one's journey.

Spirituality and ministry, likewise, cannot be construed separately any more than the idea of loving God and loving others can be understood independently of each other. One demonstrates genuine love for God by truly loving others. Conversely, when one authentically loves and serves others, he or she, in reality, is loving and serving God. Communion with God results in deep community with others. True spirituality leads to creative ministry; real ministry comes as a natural fruit of genuine spirituality. Spirituality and ministry go together and are correctly viewed as one piece.

Regarding the conjoined status of theology and spirituality, both are reckoned to relate interdependently. Knowing God means loving God, and both involve experiencing his reality in one's life. Theological impression gives way to spiritual expression in the same way that the reality of the expression itself solidifies the truth of the actual impression. In a dynamic fashion, doctrine and practice interact within the intersecting realms of both the objective and the subjective. True theology is as much a practical matter as spirituality is a genuinely lived experience; both constitute a living encounter with the living God.

The coinherence of spirituality with psychology, ministry, and theology parallels with Henri Nouwen's threefold schema of reaching out to the innermost self in solitude, reaching out to fellow human beings in service, and reaching out to God in prayer. In addition, these three interactive movements of the spiritual life correspond with the unified movement of love at the core of the Great Commandment: love of self, love of others, and love of God. These, in turn, coincide with the journey of love upon which everyone embarks: the inward journey to self, the outward journey to others, and the upward (or Godward) journey to God.

All three journeying movements toward perfection in love occur within the context of imperfect realities with which one has to wrestle. In truth, the inward, outward, and upward journeys are journeys of imperfection.

The inward journey of imperfection involves self-confrontation in conjunction with the human reality of brokenness. The path leading to wholeness is through the inward process of woundedness and brokenness. One experiences a growing sense of wholeness by first coming in direct contact with one's inner condition of brokenness.

The outward journey of imperfection represents a movement toward others within the context of ministry. Fruitfulness in ministry can only be achieved by dying to one's self and bringing an end to self's perceived power. True power in ministry is displayed best in the midst of weakness. God's power flows freely through a weak vessel.

The upward journey of imperfection has to do with the idea of reaching up to God via communion in prayer. The way to holiness incorporates the sobering experience of suffering as a preliminary to glory. Union with God means communion with and through suffering.

The realities of the inward, outward, and upward journeys show that they are anything but smooth. Indeed, the journey to perfection is through imperfection.

Henri Nouwen exemplified this threefold journeying challenge in his life—inwardly, outwardly, and upwardly. Yet, in the midst of his personal encounters with the glaring realities of imperfection associated with the experience of brokenness, weakness, and suffering, Nouwen never stopped giving of himself to others through the avenue of ministry—the ministry of soul care and spiritual formation in particular.

In a variety of ways, Henri Nouwen's multifaceted method of ministry is uniquely integrative: multilingual, multidimensional, and multidisciplinary at the same time. It undeniably reflects a holistic mindset that stems from his essential understanding of the coinherence of spirituality with the realms of psychology, ministry, and theology. Nouwen's wide engagement with the whole array of soul care and spiritual formation styles of ministry—whether it be spiritual friendship, guidance, mentoring, or direction—indicates a more generalist than a specialist approach. While assuming a multitasking mode, Nouwen demonstrates ease in seamlessly combining various elements of practical theology, counseling, psychology, pastoral care, and spiritual formation. Additionally, Henri Nouwen distinguishes his ministry approach by its counterintuitive and countercultural qualities.

Overall, Henri Nouwen's integrative mindset and approach, based on his clear grasp of the coinherence of spirituality, psychology, ministry, and theology, are both propelled and tempered by the striking reality of imperfection that he himself exemplified throughout his entire existence. Henri Nouwen stands as a perfect embodiment of a spirituality of imperfection.

He is a quintessential example of a restless, wandering soul whose energy is expended searching for himself, seeking out others and the world, and deeply longing for God. Through his endless process of restless seeking, Nouwen confronts his troubled self, his conflicted relationships with others, his disordered existence amidst an imperfect world, and his sometimes wavering relationship with God. Along the way, he shows passion and determination not to quit until he finds his final rest in God.

Born with a wounded and broken heart, Henri Nouwen wrestles throughout his life with a deep wound of loneliness that no earthly relationships can satisfy. Despite the agonizing struggle that comes with having to live with the reality of his inner wound, Nouwen devotes his energy to bringing healing to other bruised and wounded souls. In the thick of pain, Henri Nouwen emerges as the paragon of a wounded healer: a scarred yet soothing healer.

Through his endless struggle with life itself, Henri Nouwen was a model of fidelity. Many of his struggles proved brutal and were unceasingly determined to debilitate him. The mounting tension inside and around him could at times be overwhelming, beyond any kind of coping on his part. The presence of darkness could be both intimidating and paralyzing. Yet faithfulness was the single outstanding trait he exhibited to the very end.

Henri Nouwen, without a doubt, epitomizes a decidedly different brand of spirituality. Real, earthy spirituality does not obsess over perfection but willingly confronts reality as it is, with its ugly sides—including all traces of imperfection. Strangely enough, it is a spirituality that seems particularly alien to our present culture.

Spirituality and psychology, in their more contemporary expressions, are, for the most part, still enamored with skewed notions of wholeness and holiness that cast triumphal streaks. People's conceptions of spiritual ministry, impacted by heavy notions of professionalization, continue to run the risk of succumbing to the world's infatuation with success and productivity. Likewise, much of theology remains estranged from the true, vibrant practice of spirituality. For many, belief and experience still fail to connect, let alone interact dynamically.

Providentially, Henri Nouwen's writings still speak—even more loudly today—and continue to arrest many of our spiritual distortions. They beckon us to listen, but in a rather different mode: counterintuitively as well as counterculturally. G. K. Chesterton once remarked that "the saint needed by each culture is the one who contradicts it the most."[1] Henri Nouwen evidently fulfills such a role even today.

To a culture that remains highly individualistic, Henri Nouwen inculcates the ideals of community; to the narcissistic tendencies of the majority, he promotes the value of compassionate living; instead of the cherished notion of *upward* mobility with its undue emphases on success and productivity, he elevates the path of *downward* mobility with its themes of self-sacrifice and humility; to a wounded lot seeking recovery and healing, he enhances the value of *care* more than *cure* of souls; and finally, to a professedly "spiritual" generation seeking power and perfection, he introduces a theology of weakness, powerlessness, and imperfection. All in all, Henri Nouwen's spirituality is summed up simply as a spirituality of imperfection.

Notes

FOREWORD

1. Core sources: "Generation Without Fathers," *Commonweal* 92 (June 1970): 287–94; Course Lecture Notes, Spiritual Direction Class (Yale Divinity School, 1980)—adapted.

2. Henri Nouwen, *Bread for the Journey: A Daybook of Wisdom and Faith* (San Francisco: HarperSanFrancisco, 1996), July 1.

3. In my view, Nouwen's relational spirituality of imperfection is in harmony with John Wesley's approach to Christian perfection as "faith filled with the energy of love" (John Wesley, *The Works of Wesley*, 3d ed., vol. V [Grand Rapids: Baker, 1979], 497).

4. Nouwen, *Bread for the Journey*, July 1.

INTRODUCTION

1. See Henri Nouwen, *Making All Things New: An Invitation to the Spiritual Life* (San Francisco: HarperSanFrancisco, 1981), 55–56, 93. *(MN)*

2. See Henri Nouwen, *Reaching Out: The Three Movements of the Spiritual Life* (New York: Image Books, 1975), 13–14. *(RO)*

3. See Timothy George and Alister McGrath, eds., *For All the Saints: Evangelical Theology and Christian Spirituality* (Louisville, KY: Westminster John Knox Press, 2003), 3.

PART I: THE *INTEGRATED* JOURNEY

ONE: JOURNEY INWARD

1. Cf. Philip Cushman, *Constructing the Self, Constructing America* (New York: Addison-Wesley, 1995); Philip Rieff, *The Triumph of the Therapeutic: Uses of Faith After Freud* (New York: Harper & Row, 1966).

2. Robert Wuthnow, *After Heaven: Spirituality in America Since the 1950s* (Berkeley and Los Angeles: University of California Press, 1998), 3–4.

3. See Deirdre LaNoue, "Henri Nouwen and Modern American Spirituality" (PhD diss., Baylor University, 1999), i, 67, 275.

4. Michael Ford, *Wounded Prophet: A Portrait of Henri J. M. Nouwen* (New York: Doubleday, 1999), 15.

5. Gerben Heitink, *Practical Theology: History, Theory, Action Domains* (Grand Rapids: Eerdmans, 1999), 271–72.

6. Gary Collins, *The Soul Search: A Spiritual Journey to Authentic Intimacy with God* (Nashville: Thomas Nelson, 1998), 2.

7. Mark R. McMinn and Todd W. Hall, "Christian Spirituality: Introduction to Special Issue—Part 2," *Journal of Psychology and Theology* 29 (spring 2001): 3.

8. George Faller, "Psychology Versus Religion," *The Journal of Pastoral Counseling* 36 (2001): 21–22.

9. See Ernest Becker, *The Denial of Death* (New York: The Free Press, 1973), 275.

10. Cf. Robert A. Jonas, ed., *Henri Nouwen: Writings Selected with an Introduction by Robert A. Jonas* (Maryknoll, NY: Orbis Books, 1998), xxv.

11. See Mark R. McMinn and Todd W. Hall, "Introduction," in *Spiritual Formation, Counseling, and Psychotherapy* (New York: Nova Science Publishers, 2003), ix.

12. See Douglas S. Hardy, "Implicit Theologies in Psychologies: Claiming Experience as an Authoritative Source for Theologizing," *Cross Currents* 53 (fall 2003): 370–74.

13. Kyle L. Henderson, "The Reformation of Pastoral Theology in the Life and Works of Henri J. M. Nouwen" (PhD diss., Southwestern Baptist Theological Seminary, 1994), 66.

14. Henri Nouwen, "A Visit with Henri Nouwen," an interview by Todd Brennan, *The Critic* 36 (summer 1978): 47.

15. Cf. Stephen Kendrick, "In Touch with the Blessing: An Interview with Henri Nouwen," *Christian Century* (March 1993): 319.

16. Nouwen, "A Visit with Henri Nouwen," 47.

17. See Henri Nouwen, *Creative Ministry* (New York: Image Books, 1978), 59. *(CM)*

18. See Barrett W. McRay, Mark R. McMinn, Karen Wrightman, Todd D. Burnett, and Shiu-Ting Donna Ho, "What

Evangelical Pastors Want to Know about Psychology," *Journal of Psychology and Theology* 29 (2001): 91.

19. See John T. McNeill, *A History of the Cure of Souls* (New York: Harper & Brothers, 1951).

20. See Henderson, "Reformation of Pastoral Theology," 50–57. Cf. Jonas, *Henri Nouwen*, xxxvii.

21. See Eric L. Johnson and Stanton L. Jones, eds., *Psychology and Christianity: Four Views* (Downers Grove, IL: InterVarsity, 2000). See also Robert C. Roberts and Mark R. Talbot, eds., *Limning the Psyche: Explorations in Christian Psychology* (Grand Rapids: Eerdmans, 1997).

22. Siang-Yang Tan, "Intrapersonal Integration: The Servant's Spirituality," *Journal of Psychology and Christianity* 6 (1987): 34.

23. Siang-Yang Tan, "Integration and Beyond: Principled, Professional, and Personal," *Journal of Psychology and Christianity* 20 (2001): 18–28.

24. Henri Nouwen, *The Inner Voice of Love: A Journey Through Anguish to Freedom* (New York: Image Books, 1998). *(IVL)*

25. See Mark R. McMinn, *Psychology, Theology, and Spirituality in Christian Counseling* (Wheaton, IL: Tyndale House, 1996), 8, 26.

26. Everett L. Worthington, "A Blueprint for Intradisciplinary Integration," *Journal of Psychology and Theology* 22 (summer 1994): 79.

27. McMinn and Hall, "Introduction," in *Spiritual Formation*, ix.

28. Henri Nouwen, *Letters to Marc About Jesus: Living a Spiritual Life in a Material World* (San Francisco: HarperSanFrancisco, 1988), 5. *(LM)*

29. Deborah van Deusen Hunsinger, *Theology and Pastoral Counseling: A New Interdisciplinary Approach* (Grand Rapids: Eerdmans, 1998).

30. Henderson, "Reformation of Pastoral Theology," 72.

31. See Henri Nouwen, *Intimacy* (San Francisco: HarperSanFrancisco, 1969). *(I)*

32. See David G. Benner, *Care of Souls: Revisioning Christian Nurture and Counsel* (Grand Rapids: Baker, 1998), 12–13.

33. Dallas Willard, "Spiritual Disciplines, Spiritual Formation, and the Restoration of the Soul," *Journal of Psychology and Theology* 26 (1998): 101.

34. See for instance the following publications, to name a few: Jack Canfield and Mark Victor Hansen, comps., *Chicken Soup for*

the Soul: 101 Stories to Open the Heart and Rekindle the Spirit (Deerfield Beach, FL: Health Communications, 1993); Thomas Moore, *Care of the Soul* (New York: HarperCollins, 1992); Warren S. Brown, Nancey C. Murphy, and H. Newton Malony, eds., *Whatever Happened to the Soul?* (Minneapolis: Fortress Press, 1998); Michael Ventura, "Soul in the Raw: A Report from Las Vegas," *Psychology Today* 30 (May/June 1997): 58–86.

35. Collins, *The Soul Search*, 16.

36. Quoted in George Gallup, Jr., and Timothy Jones, *The NEXT American Spirituality: Finding God in the Twenty-First Century* (Colorado Springs: Victor Books, 2000), 29.

37. Willard, "Spiritual Disciplines," 108.

38. Ibid. Thus, Willard refers to such processes as *"soul re-formation"* (author's emphasis). It must be noted that the concept of the soul is still part riddle as far as a complete theological and psychological understanding of it is concerned. Scripture itself is not that crystal clear when it employs the term "soul." For this book's purposes, *soul,* as it is used here, refers to the totality of the person created in the image of God.

39. Daniel B. Wood, "Buddhist Practices Make Inroads in the U.S.," *The Christian Science Monitor* (November 3, 1997): 9.

40. Wuthnow, *After Heaven*, 142, 167.

41. Henri J. M. Nouwen, "Christian Spirituality Lecture Notes," 1972, unprocessed material (The Henri J. M. Nouwen Archives and Research Collection, John M. Kelly Library, University of St. Michael's College, Toronto), unpaginated.

42. Dallas Willard, "Spiritual Formation in Christ: A Perspective on What It Is and How It Might Be Done," *Journal of Psychology and Theology* 28 (2000): 256.

43. See Wuthnow, *After Heaven*, 150–57.

44. Henri Nouwen, "Contemplation and Action," a sermon preached at St. Paul's Church, Columbia University, December 10, 1978 (The Henri J. M. Nouwen Archives and Research Collection, John M. Kelly Library, University of St. Michael's College, Toronto), 19.

45. Jeffrey K. Hadden, "The Private Generation," *Psychology Today* 3 (October 1969): 32–35, 68–69, as cited in Henri J. M. Nouwen, "Generation Without Fathers," *Commonweal* 92 (12 June 1970): 288.

46. Paul Vitz, *Psychology as Religion: The Cult of Self-Worship* (Grand Rapids: Eerdmans, 1994), 126.

47. Ray S. Anderson, *Self Care: A Theology of Personal Empowerment & Spiritual Healing* (Wheaton, IL: Victor Books, 1995), especially chaps. 5 and 6. Cf. Jay Adams, *The Biblical View of Self-Esteem, Self-Love, Self-Image* (Eugene, OR: Harvest House Publishers, 1990).

48. Henri Nouwen, "Living in the Center Enables Us to Care," *Health Progress* (Canada) 71 (July–August 1990): 53–54.

49. James Beck, "Self and Soul," *Journal of Psychology and Theology* 26 (spring 1998): 31.

50. Stanley J. Grenz, *The Social God and the Relational Self: A Trinitarian Theology of the Imago Dei* (Louisville, KY: Westminster John Knox Press, 2001), 3.

51. Nancy S. Duvall, "From Soul to Self and Back Again," *Journal of Psychology and Theology* 26 (spring 1998): 8.

52. Grenz, *Social God*, 59.

53. Dwight H. Judy, *Christian Meditation and Inner Healing* (Akron, OH: OSL Publications, 2000), 31.

54. Michael O'Laughlin, *God's Beloved: A Spiritual Biography of Henri Nouwen* (Maryknoll, NY: Orbis Books, 2004), 163.

55. Elizabeth O'Connor, *Journey Inward, Journey Outward* (New York: Harper & Row, 1968), 13.

56. Henri Nouwen, *The Return of the Prodigal Son: A Story of Homecoming* (New York: Image Books, 1992), 16–18. *(RPS)*

57. Calvin Miller, *Into the Depths of God* (Minneapolis: Bethany House Publishers, 2000), 15.

58. Jeff Imbach, *The River Within: Loving God, Living Passionately* (Colorado Springs: NavPress, 1998), 61.

59. Philip Yancey, "Knowledge of the Journey," in *Nouwen Then: Personal Reflections on Henri*, ed. Christopher de Vinck (Grand Rapids: Zondervan, 1999), 31.

60. Henri Nouwen, *Here and Now: Living in the Spirit* (New York: Crossroad, 1994), 21. *(HN)*

61. See Ellen T. Charry, "Theology After Psychology," in *Care for the Soul*, ed. Mark R. McMinn and Timothy R. Phillips (Downers Grove, IL: InterVarsity, 2001), 125.

62. Saint Augustine, *Soliloquies: Augustine's Interior Dialogue*, trans. Kim Paffenroth (New York: New City Press, 2000), 23.

63. Rowan Williams, *The Wound of Knowledge* (London: Darton, Longman and Todd, 1979, 1990), 89.

64. See Andrew Louth, *The Origins of the Christian Mystical Tradition: From Plato to Denys* (New York: Oxford University Press, 1981), 143, 150.

65. Kendrick, "In Touch with the Blessing," 319.

66. John Calvin, *Institutes of the Christian Religion* 1.1.1, 7 (MacDill, FL: MacDonald, n.d.), quoted by James M. Houston in "The 'Double Knowledge' as the Way of Wisdom," in *The Way of Wisdom: Essays in Honor of Bruce K. Waltke*, ed. J. I. Packer and Sven K. Soderlund (Grand Rapids: Zondervan, 2000), 316.

67. James Finley, *Merton's Palace of Nowhere*, 25th anniversary ed. (Notre Dame: Ave Maria Press, 2003), 35.

68. Søren Kierkegaard, *Fear and Trembling and the Sickness Unto Death* (Princeton: Princeton University Press, 1954), 211.

69. Ronald Rolheiser, *The Holy Longing: The Search for a Christian Spirituality* (New York: Doubleday, 1999), xv.

70. Henri Nouwen, "Spiritual Direction," *Worship* 55 (September 1981): 402.

71. Henri Nouwen, *Lifesigns: Intimacy, Fecundity, and Ecstasy in Christian Perspective* (New York: Doubleday, 1986), 38. *(LS)*

72. James R. Newby and Elizabeth Newby, *Between Peril and Promise* (Nashville: Thomas Nelson, 1984), 40.

73. See Luci Shaw, *Life Path* (East Sussex, England: Christina Press, 1997), 13. Cf. Henri Nouwen, *The Genesee Diary: Report from a Trappist Monastery* (New York: Doubleday, 1976). *(GD)*

74. Benner, *Care of Souls*, 14–15.

75. Ibid., 13, 62, 110.

TWO: JOURNEY OUTWARD

1. Eugene H. Peterson, *Under the Unpredictable Plant: An Exploration in Vocational Holiness* (Grand Rapids: Eerdmans, 1992), 2–3.

2. Henri Nouwen, "Education to Ministry," *Theological Education* 9 (autumn 1972): 51.

3. I owe the basic idea for this threefold sequence from Alex B. Aronis's book *Developing Intimacy with God: An Eight-Week Prayer Guide Based on "The Spiritual Exercises of St. Ignatius"* (Makati: Union Church of Manila Phils. Foundation, 2001), 8–9.

4. See Eugene H. Peterson, "Missing Ingredient," *Christian Century* (22 March 2003): 30.

5. Henri Nouwen, *Sabbatical Journey: The Diary of His Final Year* (New York: Crossroad, 1998), 165. *(SJ)*

6. Quoted in Arthur Boers, "What Henri Nouwen Found at Daybreak: Experiments in Spiritual Living in a Secular World," *Christianity Today* (3 October 1994): 29.

7. Henri Nouwen, *¡Gracias! A Latin American Journal* (Maryknoll, NY: Orbis Books, 1993), 30. *(G!)*

8. Henri Nouwen, *The Living Reminder: Service and Prayer in Memory of Jesus Christ* (San Francisco: HarperSanFrancisco, 1977), 30–31. *(LR)*

9. See Alicia Maria Ramirez de Arellano, "Henri Nouwen Finds a Home," an interview with Henri Nouwen, *Catholic Digest* 57 (February 1993): 87.

10. A life of communion with God, Nouwen announces, "…is also a life that calls me to give all that I am in the service of [God's] love for the world" (idem, *Heart Speaks to Heart: Three Prayers to Jesus* [Notre Dame: Ave Maria Press, 1989], 43). *(HSH)*

11. Henri Nouwen, "The Monk and the Cripple: Toward a Spirituality of Ministry," *America* 142 (March 1980): 207.

12. Henri Nouwen, *With Burning Hearts: A Meditation on the Eucharistic Life* (Maryknoll, NY: Orbis Books, 2002), 75–76. *(BH)*

13. Rebecca Laird, "Parting Words: A Conversation on Prayer with Henri Nouwen," *Sacred Journey: The Journal of Fellowship in Prayer* 47 (December 1996): 13. To Nouwen, "The inner life is always a life for others" (idem, *Our Greatest Gift: A Meditation on Death and Dying* [New York: HarperCollins, 1995], 6). *(GG)*

14. Henri Nouwen, *Behold the Beauty of the Lord* (Notre Dame: Ave Maria Press, 2000), 60. *(BBL)*

15. Henri Nouwen, *Clowning in Rome: Reflections on Solitude, Celibacy, Prayer, and Contemplation* (New York: Image Books, 2000), 30. *(CR)*

16. Henri Nouwen, *In My Own Words*, comp. Robert Durback (Liguori, MO: Liguori, 2001), 128–29. Cf. idem, Clowning in Rome, 100.

17. Henri Nouwen, "What Do You Know by Heart?" *Sojourners* 6 (August 1977): 16.

18. See Elie Wiesel, "Longing for Home," in Leroy S. Rouner, ed., *The Longing for Home* (Notre Dame: University of Notre Dame Press, 1996), 19. Henri Nouwen painted a similar scenario of dislocation and rootlessness in his book *The Wounded Healer* (New York: Image Books, 1979), chaps. 1 and 2 passim. *(WH)*

19. Catherine M. Harmer, *The Compassionate Community: Strategies That Work for the Third Millennium* (Maryknoll, NY: Orbis Books, 1998), 5.

20. Parker J. Palmer, *A Place Called Community* (Philadelphia: Pendle Hill, 1977), 8.

21. Gibson Winter, *Community and Spiritual Transformation: Religion and Politics in a Communal Age* (New York: Crossroad, 1989), 29.

22. For a detailed documentation of this trend, see Robert D. Putnam, *Bowling Alone: The Collapse and Revival of American Community* (New York: Simon & Schuster, 2000), especially pp. 73 and 388.

23. Henri Nouwen, Donald P. McNeill, and Douglas A. Morrison, *Compassion: A Reflection on the Christian Life* (New York: Image Books, 1983), 50. *(C)*

24. Nouwen, "What Do You Know?," 16. Ours is always a communal calling, a common vocation (see *Clowning in Rome*, 18–19). "Together we reach out to others" (idem, *Our Greatest Gift*, 64).

25. Henri Nouwen, *The Way of the Heart: Desert Spirituality and Contemporary Ministry* (San Francisco: HarperSanFrancisco, 1991), 33. *(WOH)*

26. Jean Vanier, *Becoming Human* (Mahwah, NJ: Paulist Press, 1998), 57.

27. Ibid., 59, 62, 67.

28. Jean Vanier, *Community and Growth* (Mahwah, NJ: Paulist Press, 1979, 1989), 331.

29. Henri Nouwen, *Bread for the Journey: A Daybook of Wisdom and Faith* (San Francisco: HarperSanFrancisco, 1997), November 1. *(BJ)*

30. Dietrich Bonhoeffer, *Life Together* (San Francisco: HarperSanFrancisco, 1954), 38.

31. Henri Nouwen, "Intimacy, Fecundity, and Ecstasy," *Radix* 15 (May/June 1984): 10.

32. Nouwen also likens prayer to "the breath of the Christian community" (*Clowning in Rome*, 30–31).

33. Henri Nouwen, "Where You Would Rather Not Go" (commencement address, June 2, 1981, Princeton Theological Seminary) *Princeton Seminary Bulletin*, n.s. 3 (1982): 239.

34. Lorenzo Sforza-Cesarini, interview by author, tape recording, Richmond Hill, Ontario, 28 April 2004.

35. Henri Nouwen, *With Open Hands: Bringing Prayer into Your Life* (New York: Ballantine Books, 1985), 49. *(OH)*

36. Henri Nouwen, *Life of the Beloved: Spiritual Living in a Secular World* (New York: Crossroad, 1992), 63. (*LOB*)

37. See Laird, "Parting Words," 17.

38. Elie Wiesel, "The Refuge," *Cross Currents* 34 (winter 1984): 386.

39. Larry Rasmussen, "Shaping Communities," in *Practicing Our Faith: A Way of Life for a Searching People*, ed. Dorothy C. Bass (San Francisco: Jossey-Bass, 1997), 120.

40. Marva J. Dawn, *Truly the Community: Romans 12 and How to Be the Church* (Grand Rapids: Eerdmans, 2000), 81.

41. Christine D. Pohl, "A Community's Practice of Hospitality: The Interdependence of Practices and of Communities," in *Practicing Theology: Beliefs and Practices in Christian Life*, ed. Miroslav Volf and Dorothy C. Bass (Grand Rapids: Eerdmans, 2002), 135. See also Pohl's book *Making Room: Recovering Hospitality as a Christian Tradition* (Grand Rapids: Eerdmans, 1999).

42. Nouwen, "Education to Ministry," 49.

43. Dawn, *Truly the Community*, 214.

44. Nouwen, "Education to Ministry," 71.

45. Robert C. Morris, "Fear or Fascination? God's Call in a Multicultural World," *Weavings: A Journal of the Christian Spiritual Life* 18 (September/October 2003): 18.

46. Nouwen, "Education to Ministry," 50.

47. Rolheiser, *Holy Longing*, 53, 64–66. Cf. Glen H. Stassen and David P. Gushee, *Kingdom Ethics: Following Jesus in Contemporary Context* (Downers Grove, IL: InterVarsity, 2003), 355–65.

48. Gustavo Gutiérrez, *A Theology of Liberation*, rev. ed. (London: SCM Press, 1998), 118.

49. Brian V. Johnstone, "The Dynamics of Conversion," in *Spirituality and Morality: Integrating Prayer and Action*, ed. Dennis J. Billy and Donna Lynn Orsuto (Mahwah, NJ: Paulist Press, 1996), 46.

50. Henri Nouwen, "Nuclear Man: In Search for Liberation," *Reflection* 70 (November 1972): unpaginated.

51. Margaret R. Miles, *Practicing Christianity: Critical Perspectives for an Embodied Spirituality* (New York: Crossroad, 1990), 118–20.

52. See Stassen and Gushee, *Kingdom Ethics*, 229; see especially chap. 16, where Stassen expounds in moving detail the example of the compassionate Samaritan (Luke 10:25–37), 327–42.

53. Ford, *Wounded Prophet*, 53. For more on Nouwen's peace and justice initiatives, see Henri Nouwen, *The Road to Peace*, ed. John Dear (Maryknoll, NY: Orbis Books, 1998). *(RP)*

54. See Henri Nouwen, "Prayer and Health Care," *CHAC Review* 17 (winter 1989): 11–16.

55. See Beth Porter with Susan S. Brown and Philip Coulter, eds., *Befriending Life: Encounters with Henri Nouwen* (New York: Doubleday, 2001) and de Vinck, ed., *Nouwen Then*.

56. See Nouwen, "A Visit with Henri Nouwen," 46.

57. Jay M. Uomoto, "Human Suffering, Psychotherapy and Soul Care: The Spirituality of Henri J. M. Nouwen at the Nexus," *Journal of Psychology and Christianity* 14 (winter 1995): 347, 352.

58. Henri Nouwen, *From Resentment to Gratitude* (Chicago: Franciscan Herald Press, 1974), 30.

59. Nouwen, "A Visit with Henri Nouwen," 45.

60. John Macquarrie, *Paths in Spirituality* (London: SCM Press, 1972), 72.

61. David G. Benner, *Surrender to Love: Discovering the Heart of Christian Spirituality* (Downers Grove, IL: InterVarsity, 2003), 28.

62. Owen C. Thomas, "Interiority and Christian Spirituality," *The Journal of Religion* 80 (January 2000): 41.

63. Ibid. 42, 60.

64. See Miles, *Practicing Christianity*.

65. Henri Nouwen, foreword to *We Drink from Our Own Wells: The Spiritual Journey of a People*, by Gustavo Gutiérrez (Maryknoll, NY: Orbis Books, 1984), xvi.

66. Kenneth Leech, "'Let the Oppressed Go Free': Spiritual Direction and the Pursuit of Justice," in *Still Listening: New Horizons in Spiritual Direction*, ed. Norvene Vest (Harrisburg, PA: Morehouse Publishing, 2000), 123.

67. Dennis J. Billy, "The Unfolding of a Tradition," in Billy and Orsuto, *Spirituality and Morality*, 21.

68. Dennis Hollinger, *Choosing the Good: Christian Ethics in a Complex World* (Grand Rapids: Baker, 2002), 12–13.

69. Thomas, "Interiority," 55.

70. Jurgen Beumer, *Henri Nouwen: A Restless Seeking for God* (New York: Crossroad, 1997), n. 22, p. 180.

71. Segundo Galilea, "The Spirituality of Liberation," *The Way* (July 1985): 186–94, cited in Philip Sheldrake, *Spaces for the Sacred: Place, Memory and Identity* (London: SCM Press, 2002), 137–38.

72. Henri Nouwen, foreword to *The Way of Living Faith: A Spirituality of Liberation*, by Segundo Galilea (San Francisco: Harper & Row, 1988), ix. For Nouwen, "action and contemplation are two sides of the same reality" (*Creative Ministry*, 88).

73. Henri Nouwen, "Contemplation and Ministry," *Sojourners* 7 (June 1978): 9.

74. Sheldrake, *Spaces for the Sacred*, 93–94.

75. Ibid., 99–101.

76. Ibid., 128.

77. Philip Sheldrake, "Christian Spirituality as a Way of Living Publicly: A Dialectic of the Mystical and Prophetic," *Spiritus: A Journal of Christian Spirituality* 3 (spring 2003): 19, 23.

THREE: JOURNEY UPWARD

1. See, for instance, D. A. Carson, *The Gagging of God: Christianity Confronts Pluralism* (Grand Rapids: Zondervan, 1996), 555–69.

2. Alister E. McGrath, *Christian Spirituality: An Introduction* (Oxford: Blackwell, 1999), 25.

3. George Lindbeck, foreword to *By the Renewing of Your Minds: The Pastoral Function of Christian Doctrine*, by Ellen T. Charry (New York: Oxford University Press, 1997), xiii.

4. Charry, *Renewing of Your Minds*, 240.

5. Parker J. Palmer, *To Know As We Are Known: Education As a Spiritual Journey* (San Francisco: HarperSanFrancisco, 1993), xv.

6. Henri Nouwen, *Show Me the Way: Readings for Each Day of Lent*, ed. Franz Johna (New York: Crossroad, 1992), 108.

7. John Calvin, *Institutes of the Christian Religion* 1.5.9, trans. Ford Lewis Battles (Philadelphia: Westminster Press, 1960).

8. William C. Placher, *The Domestication of Transcendence: How Modern Thinking about God Went Wrong* (Louisville, KY: Westminster John Knox Press, 1996), n. 13, p. 54.

9. Charry, *Renewing of Your Minds*, 239.

10. Philip Sheldrake, *Spirituality and Theology: Christian Living and the Doctrine of God* (Maryknoll, NY: Orbis Books, 1998), 15.

11. Ibid., 100.

12. Joan Nuth, *God's Lovers in an Age of Anxiety: The Medieval English Mystics* (New York: Orbis Books, 2001), 22.

13. See Teresa of Ávila, *The Interior Castle*, trans. Kieran Kavanaugh and Otilio Rodriguez (Mahwah, NJ: Paulist Press, 1979), 9.

14. James J. Bacik, *Catholic Spirituality, Its History and Challenge* (Mahwah, NJ: Paulist Press, 2002), 20, 23.

15. J. Matthew Ashley, "The Turn to Spirituality? The Relationship Between Theology and Spirituality," *Christian Spirituality Bulletin* 3 (fall 1995): 15.

16. Henri Nouwen, "Theology as Doxology: Reflections on Theological Education," in *Caring for the Commonweal: Education for Religious and Public Life*, ed. Parker J. Palmer, Barbara G.

Wheeler, and James W. Fowler (Macon, Georgia: Mercer University Press, 1990), 94.

17. See, in particular, Henri Nouwen, *Spiritual Journals: Three Books in One* (New York: Continuum, 1997). In Sue Mosteller's ironic description, Nouwen was "a man of tremendous contradiction and integration at the same time" (interview by author, tape recording, Richmond Hill, Ontario, 26 April 2004).

18. Jean Vanier, "A Gentle Instrument of a Loving God," in *Befriending Life*, 266.

19. Henri Nouwen, "Simple Joys," *Other Side* 144 (September 1983): 49.

20. Bacik, *Catholic Spirituality*, 49.

21. Robert Waldron, *Walking with Henri Nouwen: A Reflective Journey* (Mahwah, NJ: Paulist Press, 2003), 67.

22. Henri Nouwen, *Can You Drink the Cup?* (Notre Dame: Ave Maria Press, 1996), 26–27. *(CYD)*

23. See Ford, *Wounded Prophet*, 67.

24. Mary Frohlich, "Spiritual Discipline, Discipline of Spirituality: Revisiting Questions of Definition and Method," *Spiritus* 1 (spring 2001): 68.

25. Eugene Peterson, as cited in *Christian Century* (18 October 2003): 5.

26. Alister E. McGrath, *The Future of Christianity* (Oxford: Blackwell, 2002), 137.

27. See Sandra M. Schneiders, "The Study of Christian Spirituality: Contours and Dynamics of a Discipline," *Christian Spirituality Bulletin* 6 (spring 1998): 10.

28. McGrath, *Christian Spirituality*, 10.

29. See Edward Farley, *Theologia: The Fragmentation and Unity of Theological Education* (Philadelphia: Fortress Press, 1983) as quoted in McGrath, *Christian Spirituality*, 27–28.

30. Nouwen, "Theology as Doxology," 96.

31. Quoted in Eric O. Springsted, ed., *Spirituality and Theology: Essays in Honor of Diogenes Allen* (Louisville, KY: Westminster John Knox Press, 1998), 8.

32. Nouwen, "Theology as Doxology," 96.

33. Ford, *Wounded Prophet*, 9.

34. Kenneth Leech, *Experiencing God: Theology as Spirituality* (New York: Harper & Row, 1985), vii.

35. Ford, *Wounded Prophet*, 9; also p. 8.

36. See Beumer, *Henri Nouwen*, 140–41. For more on Nouwen's creative and artistic method of doing theology, see O'Laughlin, *God's Beloved*, chap. 3, pp. 86–109.

37. Sheldrake, *Spirituality and Theology*, 3.

38. For sample definitions of Christian spirituality, see Lawrence S. Cunningham and Keith J. Egan, *Christian Spirituality: Themes from the Tradition* (Mahwah, NJ: Paulist Press, 1996), 22–28.

39. Mark Buchanan, "We're All Syncretists Now: Not Religious, Just Spiritual," *Books and Culture: A Christian Review* 6 (January/February 2000): 10.

40. Philip Sheldrake, *Spirituality and History: Questions of Interpretation and Method*, new ed. (New York: Orbis Books, 1995), 40, 45.

41. McGrath, *Future of Christianity*, 135–36. Author's emphasis is in the original.

42. Bernard McGinn, "The Letter and the Spirit: Spirituality as an Academic Discipline," *Christian Spirituality Bulletin* 1 (fall 1993): 1–10, as cited in Sheldrake, *Spirituality and Theology*, 85.

43. See Sandra M. Schneiders, "Theology and Spirituality: Strangers, Rivals, or Partners?" *Horizons* 13 (fall 1986): 253–74.

44. Sheldrake, *Spirituality and Theology*, 32; pp. 85, 87–95.

45. Mark A. McIntosh, *Mystical Theology: The Integrity of Spirituality and Theology* (Oxford: Blackwell, 1998), 6.

46. Henri Nouwen, *In the Name of Jesus: Reflections on Christian Leadership* (New York: Crossroad, 1989), 30. *(INJ)*

47. Henri Nouwen, *The Road to Daybreak: A Spiritual Journey* (New York: Doubleday, 1988), 120. *(RD)*

48. Timothy George, "Traveling Mercies," *Vocatio* (spring 2001): unpaginated. Cf. William Ames, *The Marrow of Theology*, ed. John D. Eusden (Boston: Pilgrim Press, 1968), 77.

49. Bruce Demarest, *Satisfy Your Soul: Restoring the Heart of Christian Spirituality* (Colorado Springs: NavPress, 1999), 84, 120.

50. Bacik, *Catholic Spirituality*, 8. This is especially true for Eastern Christianity: "The East has managed to preserve…the organic connection between theology and spirituality" as exemplified in Origen's united vision of integrating "biblical exegesis, theological reflection and spiritual wisdom" (p. 11).

51. Louth, *The Origins of the Christian Mystical Tradition*, xii.

52. Bacik, *Catholic Spirituality*, 6.

53. McGrath, *Future of Christianity*, 137.

54. See Marva Dawn, "Practiced Theology—Lived Spirituality," in *For All the Saints*, ed. George and McGrath, 137–54.

55. Richard J. Mouw, *Consulting the Faithful: What Christian Intellectuals Can Learn from Popular Religion* (Grand Rapids: Eerdmans, 1994), 69. Cf. Nouwen, *In the Name of Jesus*, 67–68.

56. Beumer, *Henri Nouwen*, 142.

57. Robert Durback, *A Retreat with Nouwen: Reclaiming Our Humanity* (Cincinnati: St. Anthony Messenger Press, 2003), 5.

58. Quoted in Ford, *Wounded Prophet*, 113.

59. Henri Nouwen, *Adam: God's Beloved* (Maryknoll, NY: Orbis Books, 1997), 50. *(A)*

60. Nouwen, "Theology as Doxology," 109.

61. Annice Callahan, "Henri Nouwen: The Heart as Home," in *Spiritualities of the Heart: Approaches to Personal Wholeness in Christian Tradition*, ed. Annice Callahan (Mahwah, NJ: Paulist Press, 1990), 205.

62. See Jose Panachimootil, "Heart Centered Spirituality for Ministers: The Life and Writings of Henri J. M. Nouwen" (Pars dissertationis ad lauream in Facultae S. Theologae apud Pontificiam Universitatem S. Thomae in Urbe, Romae: [s.n.], 2000), 87.

PART II: THE *IMPERFECT* JOURNEY

FOUR: SPIRITUALITY OF IMPERFECTION

1. See Ray S. Anderson, *On Being Human: Essays in Theological Anthropology* (Pasadena, CA: Fuller Seminary Press, 1982), 214.

2. Ibid., 206; see also 31–32.

3. Rebecca Laird and Michael J. Christensen, *The Heart of Nouwen: His Words of Blessing* (New York: Crossroad, 2003), 131.

4. Frederick Buechner, *The Longing for Home: Recollections and Reflections* (New York: HarperCollins, 1996), 109–10. See Nouwen, *Life of the Beloved*, 75.

5. Cornelius Plantinga, Jr., *Not the Way It's Supposed to Be: A Breviary of Sin* (Grand Rapids: Eerdmans, 1995), 10.

6. Henri Nouwen, *Finding My Way Home: Pathways to Life and the Spirit* (New York: Crossroad, 2001), 81. *(FWH)*

7. Jonas, *Henri Nouwen*, lxvii.

8. See Larry Crabb, *Understanding Who You Are: What Your Relationships Tell You About Yourself* (Colorado Springs: NavPress, 1997), 47.

9. Laird and Christensen, *Heart of Nouwen*, 14. The aphorism "we become what we love" was true for Nouwen (Jonas, *Henri Nouwen*, lxviii).

10. Karl Barth, *Church Dogmatics*, IV/1 (Edinburgh: T. & T. Clark, Sons, 1956), 190, as quoted in Nouwen, *Compassion*, 27.

11. Timothy B. Savage, *Power Through Weakness: Paul's Understanding of the Christian Ministry in 2 Corinthians* (Cambridge: Cambridge University Press, 1996), 185–86.

12. Nouwen, "Monk and the Cripple," 207, 205.

13. Philip Sheldrake, *Images of Holiness: Explorations in Contemporary Spirituality* (Notre Dame: Ave Maria Press, 1988), 44.

14. Marva J. Dawn, *Powers, Weakness, and the Tabernacling of God* (Grand Rapids: Eerdmans, 2001), 47. In her careful exegesis and brilliant exposition of 2 Corinthians 11:30 and 12:7–10, Dawn concludes: "The goal is for *our* [emphasis mine] power to come to its end" so God's power can be highlighted all the more" (p. 41).

15. Michael J. Gorman, *Cruciformity: Paul's Narrative Spirituality of the Cross* (Grand Rapids: Eerdmans, 2001), 293.

16. Donald L. Alexander, ed., *Christian Spirituality: Five Views of Sanctification* (Downers Grove, IL: InterVarsity, 1988), 7.

17. J. Robertson McQuilkin, "The Keswick Perspective," in Melvin E. Dieter et al., *Five Views on Sanctification* (Grand Rapids: Zondervan, 1987), 153.

18. Sheldrake, *Images of Holiness*, 28–29.

19. J. I. Packer, *Keep in Step with the Spirit* (Old Tappan, NJ: Revell, 1984), 111.

20. Ron Julian, *Righteous Sinners: The Believer's Struggle with Faith, Grace, and Works* (Colorado Springs: NavPress, 1998), 173.

21. Henri Nouwen, *A Cry for Mercy: Prayers from the Genesee* (New York: Image Books, 2002), 123. *(CFM)*

22. Henri Nouwen, "Rublev's *Icon of the Trinity*: A Reflection on the Spiritual Life," *Harvard Divinity Bulletin* 14 (June–August 1984): 9; idem, *Behold the Beauty*, 24.

23. See Henri Nouwen, "Living the Spiritual Life: An Interview with Henri Nouwen," by Catherine Walsh, *Saint Anthony Messenger* 93 (April 1986): 11–15.

24. As Michael O'Laughlin describes him, Nouwen was "a man of sorrows walking his own personal *via dolorosa*" (*God's Beloved*, 7).

25. Simone Weil, *Gravity and Grace*, intro. Gustve Thibon, trans. Arthur Wills (New York: G. P. Putnam's Sons, 1952), 132.

26. Henri Nouwen, *Turn My Mourning into Dancing: Finding Hope in Hard Times*, comp. and ed. Timothy Jones (Nashville: Word Publishing, 2001), 9.

27. Ibid., xv.

28. From Jean Vanier's eulogy during Nouwen's funeral in Holland as quoted by Sue Mosteller in Nouwen, *Sabbatical Journey*, ix.

29. Waldron, *Walking with Henri Nouwen*, 4.

30. John Sullivan, "To Pray and Reflect with Edith Stein," *Spiritual Life: A Journal of Contemporary Spiritual Life* (spring 2004): 35–36.

31. David Peterson, *Possessed by God: A New Testament Theology of Sanctification and Holiness* (Grand Rapids: Eerdmans, 1995), 114, 118.

32. Augustine of Hippo, *Prayers from the Confessions*, ed. John E. Rotelle (New York: New City Press, 2003), 139.

33. Henri Nouwen, *Walk with Jesus: Stations of the Cross* (Maryknoll, NY: Orbis Books, 1990), 29. *(WJ)*

34. Michael Ford, ed., *Eternal Seasons: A Liturgical Journey with Henri J. M. Nouwen* (Notre Dame: Sorin Books, 2004), 100.

35. Ed Wojcicki, "With an Open Heart, the Journey Is Simpler," in *Nouwen Then*, 125.

36. John R.W. Stott, *The Message of the Sermon on the Mount* (Downers Grove, IL: InterVarsity, 1978), 122.

37. Stassen and Gushee, *Kingdom Ethics*, 141.

38. Wilkie Au and Noreen Cannon, *Urgings of the Heart: A Spirituality of Integration* (Mahwah, NJ: Paulist Press, 1995), 75.

39. Gregory S. Clapper, *As If the Heart Mattered: A Wesleyan Spirituality* (Nashville: Upper Room Books, 1997), 73.

40. Albert C. Outler, "John Wesley as Theologian—Then and Now," *A. M. E. Zion Quarterly Review: Methodist History News Bulletin* 12 (July 1974): 76.

41. Terrence G. Kardong, "Benedict's Puzzling Theme of Perfection," *The Asbury Theological Journal* 50/51 (fall 1995/spring 1996): 38.

42. Au and Cannon, *Urgings of the Heart*, 75.

43. Thomas Merton, *Life and Holiness* (New York: Image Books, 1964), 119.

44. Wilkie Au, *The Enduring Heart: Spirituality for the Long Haul* (Mahwah, NJ: Paulist Press, 2000), 15.

45. For a brief evaluation of the merits as well as the problematic issues involved in the traditional usage of the ascent and ladder metaphors, see Miles, *Practicing Christianity*, 63–79.

46. See Richard Rohr, *The Spirituality of Imperfection* (Cincinnati: St. Anthony Messenger Press, 1997), audiocassette.

47. Charles Ringma, *Dare to Journey with Henri Nouwen* (Metro Manila: OMF Literature Inc., 1995), Reflection 66.

48. Sheldrake, *Images of Holiness*, 22.

49. Waldron, *Walking with Henri Nouwen*, 9.

50. Deirdre LaNoue, *The Spiritual Legacy of Henri Nouwen* (New York: Continuum, 2000), 108.

51. Michael Yaconelli, *Messy Spirituality: God's Annoying Love for Imperfect People* (Grand Rapids: Zondervan, 2002), 13.

52. Philip Yancey, "Honest Church Marketing," *Christianity Today* (22 October 2001): 112.

53. Williams, *Wound of Knowledge*, 182.

54. Donald McCullough, *The Consolations of Imperfection: Learning to Appreciate Life's Limitations* (Grand Rapids: Brazos Press, 2004), 78.

55. See Patricia H. Livingston, *This Blessed Mess: Finding Hope Amidst Life's Chaos* (Notre Dame: Sorin Books, 2000), 9.

56. Reinhold Niebuhr, *The Nature and Destiny of Man: A Christian Interpretation*, One-Volume Edition, vol. 2 (New York: Charles Scribner's Sons, 1941, 1943, 1949), 298.

57. Ernest Kurtz and Katherine Ketcham, *The Spirituality of Imperfection: Storytelling and the Journey to Wholeness* (New York: Bantam Books, 1994), 2, 18, 19.

58. Simon Tugwell, *Ways of Imperfection: An Exploration of Christian Spirituality* (Springfield, IL: Templegate Publishers, 1985), 8.

59. Perhaps in the course of examining Nouwen's life and spirituality more closely, we might be able to make more sense of poet Wallace Stevens's strange metaphor: "The imperfect is our paradise" (quoted in Philip Simmons, *Learning to Fall: The Blessings of an Imperfect Life* [New York: Bantam Books, 2002], 32).

FIVE: A PERFECT EXAMPLE OF IMPERFECTION

1. Philip Yancey, "Living with Furious Opposites," *Christianity Today* (4 September 2000): 80.

2. Robert Durback, ed., *Seeds of Hope: A Henri Nouwen Reader* (New York: Bantam Books, 1989), xxix.

3. Henri Nouwen, *Beyond the Mirror: Reflections on Death and Life* (New York: Crossroad, 2001), 49. (*BM*)

4. See Henri Nouwen, *Love in a Fearful Land: A Guatemalan Story* (Notre Dame: Ave Maria Press, 1985).

5. Douglas Burton-Christie, "A Sense of Place," *The Way* 39 (1999): 62.

6. Sheldrake, *Spaces for the Sacred*, 10.

7. Belden Lane, *Landscapes of the Sacred: Geography and Narrative in American Spirituality* (Mahwah, NJ: Paulist Press, 1988), 28.

8. Douglas Burton-Christie, "Living Between Two Worlds: Home, Journey and the Quest for Sacred Place" *Anglican Theological Review* 79 (summer 1997): 415.

9. See Ford, *Wounded Prophet*, 214. Cf. Nouwen, *Sabbatical Journey*, 89.

10. Burton-Christie, "Living Between Two Worlds," 416–17. Cf. Gaston Bachelard, *The Poetics of Space* (Boston: Beacon Press, 1959), 4–5, 91.

11. Cited in a video interview by Karen Pascal, *Straight to the Heart: The Life of Henri Nouwen* (Markham, ON: Windborne Productions, 2001). See also Ford, *Wounded Prophet*, 186.

12. Michel de Certeau, "The Weakness of Believing: From the Body to Writing, a Christian Transit," in *The Certeau Reader*, ed. Graham Ward, (Oxford: Blackwell, 2000), 215, as quoted in Sheldrake, *Spaces for the Sacred*, 104, 64.

13. Deborah Tall, *From Where We Stand: Recovering a Sense of Place* (New York: Knopf, 1993), 89.

14. Jonas, *Henri Nouwen*, xxxiv.

15. Burton-Christie, "Living Between Two Worlds," 421.

16. Robert M. Hamma, *Landscapes of the Soul: A Spirituality of Place* (Notre Dame: Ave Maria Press, 1999), 70.

17. Peterson, *Under the Unpredictable Plant*, 148.

18. Michael O' Laughlin, introduction to *Jesus: A Gospel*, by Henri Nouwen (Maryknoll, NY: Orbis Books, 2001), xiv. Nouwen shared about his beginning struggles in L'Arche in *Road to Daybreak*, 150, 154, 192.

19. Sarah Koops Vanderveen, "Places in the Heart," *Mars Hill Review* 20 (2003): 7. See Frederick Buechner, *The Longing for Home: Recollections and Reflections* (New York: HarperCollins, 1996), 2–3.

20. Vanderveen, "Places in the Heart," 7. Or as Belden Lane puts it, "We *are* what our places make of us" ("Merton's Hermitage: Bachelard, Domestic Space, and Spiritual Transformation," *Spiritus* 4 [fall 2004]: 145). Place does function critically in identity formation.

21. See Donald Capps and Walter H. Capps, eds., *The Religious Personality* (Belmont, CA: Wadsworth, 1970), 6–7.

22. See O'Laughlin, *God's Beloved*, 143.

23. Ronald Rolheiser, *The Restless Heart: Finding Our Spiritual Home* (New York: Doubleday, 2004), ix.

24. C. S. Lewis, *A Mind Awake: An Anthology of C. S. Lewis*, ed. Clyde S. Kilby (New York: Harcourt Brace & Company, 1968), 22.

25. Timothy Jones, Preface to *Turn My Mourning* by Nouwen, xi.

26. Ford, *Wounded Prophet* 8; also 44, 50.

27. See Waldron, *Walking with Henri Nouwen*, 49, 67.

28. Henri Nouwen, foreword to *Van Gogh and God*, by Cliff Edwards (Chicago: Loyola University Press, 1989), x.

29. Henri Nouwen, *A Letter of Consolation* (San Francisco: HarperSanFrancisco, 1982), 24.

30. Rolheiser, *Restless Heart*, 3.

31. Vera Phillips and Edwin Robertson, *The Wounded Healer* (London: SPCK, 1984), vii–viii.

32. Henri Nouwen and Walter J. Gaffney, *Aging: The Fulfillment of Life* (New York: Image Books, 1990), 97.

33. John McFarland, "The Minister as Narrator," *The Christian Ministry* 189 (January 1987): 20.

34. Nathan Ball, interview by author, tape recording, Richmond Hill, Ontario, 28 April 2004.

35. John Garvey, ed., *Circles of Love: Daily Readings with Henri J. M. Nouwen* (London: Darton, Longman and Todd, 1988), ix.

36. Carolyn Whitney-Brown, "Safe in God's Heart," *Sojourners* 25 (November/December 1996): 32.

37. Ed Wojcicki, "Dear Henri: About Those Feelings," *Catholic Times*, 30 November 1986, 4.

38. Marci Whitney-Schenck, "The Wounded Healer," *Christianity and the Arts* (spring 1999): 8.

39. Kendrick, "In Touch with the Blessing," 320.

40. J. I. Packer has written an exegetically sound defense identifying the first person singular in Romans 7:7–25 with Paul, which is the interpretation I happen to subscribe to (see Packer, *Keep in Step with the Spirit*, app., pp. 263–70).

41. C. E. B. Cranfield, *The Epistle to the Romans*, The International Critical Commentary, ed. J. A. Emerton and C. E. B. Cranfield, vol. 1 (Edinburgh: T. & T. Clark, 1975), 356.

42. Merton, *Life and Holiness*, 29.

43. Sue Mosteller, foreword to *Sabbatical Journey*, ix.

44. See Henri Nouwen, *Discovering Our Gift Through Service to Others: A Conversation with Reverend Henri J. M. Nouwen* (Washington, D.C.: FADICA, 1994), 15.

45. See Peterson, *Possessed by God*, 114.

46. James D. G. Dunn, *The Theology of PAUL the Apostle* (Grand Rapids: Eerdmans, 1998), 465.

47. David Wenham, "The Christian Life: A Life of Tension?" in *Pauline Studies*, ed. Donald A. Hagner and Murray J. Harris (Grand Rapids: Eerdmans, 1980), 90.

48. People who knew Nouwen well have observed this phenomena at work in him. For instance, Joe Vorstermans spoke of how centered Nouwen was at the core of his being despite his restlessness (interview by author, tape recording, Richmond Hill, Ontario, 28 April 2004). Similarly, Wendy Lywood commented about how good Nouwen was at focusing and listening even though he appeared "scattered" sometimes (interview by author, tape recording, Richmond Hill, Ontario, 29 April 2004).

49. The way Michael O'Laughlin explains it, "Henri developed an ability to work with his limitations and integrate or 'befriend' them" (*God's Beloved*, 84).

50. Douglas Kelly, Hugh McClure, and Philip B. Rollinson, eds., *The Westminster Confession of Faith*, new ed. (Greenwood, SC: The Attic Press, 1979), chap. 18, pp. 28–29.

51. Gerald G. May, *The Dark Night of the Soul: A Psychiatrist Explores the Connection Between Darkness and Spiritual Growth* (San Francisco: HarperSanFrancisco, 2004), 4–5; 47.

52. Constance Fitzgerald, "Impasse and Dark Night," in *Women's Spirituality: Resources for Christian Development*, ed. Joann Wolski Conn (Mahwah, NJ: Paulist Press, 1986), 291.

53. Wendy Wright, as quoted in Dan Wakefield, *Spiritually Incorrect: Finding God in All the Wrong Places* (Woodstock, VT: Skylight Paths Publishing, 2004), 19–20.

54. Nathan Ball, "A Covenant of Friendship," in *Befriending Life*, 95.

55. See Robert Durback, "Henri Nouwen: Memories of a Wounded Prophet," *America* 181 (3–10 July 1999): 16–17.

56. Ibid., 17.

57. See Philip Yancey, *Soul Survivor: How My Faith Survived the Church* (New York: Doubleday, 2001), 302.

58. Robert Durback, foreword to *Beyond the Mirror*, 10.

59. Ford, *Wounded Prophet*, xv.

60. Carolyn Whitney-Brown, introduction to the memorial edition of *The Road to Daybreak*, by Henri Nouwen (London: Darton, Longman and Todd, 1977), xii, as quoted in Ford, *Wounded Prophet*, xv.

61. Rolheiser, *The Holy Longing*.

62. Waldron, *Walking with Jesus*, 86.

63. Jonas, *Henri Nouwen*, xiv.

64. Henri Nouwen, *Jesus and Mary: Finding Our Sacred Center* (Cincinnati, OH: St. Anthony Messenger Press, 1993), 30.

65. Philip Yancey, "The Holy Inefficiency of Henri Nouwen," *Christianity Today* (9 December 1996): 80.

CONCLUSION

1. Cited in Mark S. Burrows, "Gospel Fantasy," *Christian Century* (1 June 2004): 23.

PRAISE for *Henri Nouwen: A Spirituality of Imperfection*

"I enthusiastically endorse this important and wonderfully readable book. It not only provides a helpful discussion of the essential elements of the spirituality that lies at the core of Nouwen's writing but more important, makes clear how Nouwen lived this spirituality and how we can as well. As a perfect example of an imperfect saint, Nouwen invites us to join him in a spirituality of imperfection—a spirituality Wil Hernandez understands and uses as the framework for this book that is sure to be as appreciated by others as it already is by me."

David G. Benner, PhD,
author of *The Gift of Being Yourself,
Surrender to Love,* and *Care of Souls*

"Wil Hernandez has done a remarkable job of unpacking Henri Nouwen's authentic understanding of spirituality, organizing Nouwen's thinking into clear categories without in any measure sacrificing its passionate impact. Reading Wil's book (which is both scholarly and readable, in itself a noteworthy achievement) humbled me into deeper realism about my imperfections, excited me with richer awareness of Christ's love, and challenged me to pursue more bravely a spiritual journey that builds on theology, draws on psychology, and releases me to impact others."

Larry Crabb, PhD, psychologist and author,
and director of NewWay Ministries

"Henri Nouwen taught us to see beauty and grace in imperfection. Wil Hernandez' fine book gives us a thoughtful, critical introduction to this still-important spiritual vision."

Douglas Burton-Christie, PhD, Loyola Marymount University

"Wil Hernandez has given us an in-depth analysis demonstrating in Nouwen's life and writing two seemingly contradictory things: *integration* and *imperfection*. It is an important addition to the growing literature on Nouwen."

Jeff Imbach, president of Henri Nouwen Society (Canada)

"Wil Hernandez shows us that to be with Henri Nouwen in the classroom, in spiritual direction, or in the midst of a march for peace, was to encounter a holy imperfection. This book leads us into the center of that imperfection, helping us trace not only the complex contours of Henri's heart, but the contours of our own as well."

Andrew Dreitcer, PhD, director of Spiritual Formation, Claremont School of Theology

"Nouwen readers won't want to miss these keen observations of his innovative mingling of psychology, ministry, and theology and how this created an astonishing authenticity in Nouwen's writing and life."

Jan Johnson, author of *When the Soul Listens* and *Savoring God's Word*

"It is a special joy to see Henri Nouwen 'whole' in this scholarly and yet truly pastoral work of Wil Hernandez. It is a very informative and thought-provoking book about 'integration' which, as Wil makes clear, is an ongoing, never-finished project for the 'restless searcher' Henri Nouwen, and for each of us who share his God-drawn search."

Thomas H. Green, SJ, San Jose Seminary, Quezon City, Philippines

"This book serves as an inspirational challenge to live the kind of authentic spirituality so impressively modeled by Nouwen, one that Dr. Hernandez has aptly identified as a 'spirituality of imperfection.' The author gives fresh and very helpful insight into our understanding and practice of biblical spirituality. I highly recommend it."

Alex B. Aronis, PhD, pastor emeritus, Union Church of Manila and author of *Developing Intimacy with God*

"Profound and relevant. The author has written a substantive work on the holistic and integrative approach of Henri Nouwen to Christian spirituality. An excellent read, especially for the wounded healers."

Dr. Jun Vencer, vice president of Leadership Development, DAWN Ministries

"Wil Hernandez's offering to the global faith community is a Spirit-infused guidebook for renewal of our faith, of our lives, and our serving the world together in Jesus' name. At a time of growing spiritual malaise, Wil interprets Nouwen's humble life in Christ as a much-needed corrective and inspiration to us all."

Rev. Dr. Ken Fong, senior pastor of Evergreen Baptist Church of Los Angeles

"This work has captured the heart of Henri Nouwen's spiritual journey by weaving together the threads of spirituality, psychology, ministry, and theology. A must-read for anyone seeking to understand and experience the fullness of what it means to live out the Christian life."

Dr. Henry Tan, president of International School of Leadership

SPECIAL THANKS
to my faithful spiritual companions in the journey

Paul Jensen and *Alan Fadling*
and Generation 14 of The Journey
(The Leadership Institute)

Bob Howey and *Karl Bruce*
(Spiritual Formation Alliance)
and the
SoCal Spiritual Formation Network

Scott and *Kirsten, Jon* and *Scott V.*
(Ignatian Group at Fuller)

Pastoral/Ministry Staff
and my
Spiritual Formation Groups
(Evergreen Baptist Church of Los Angeles)

Academy 19 Participants
(Academy for Spiritual Formation)
especially my Covenant Group:
*Kent, Suzanne, Paulette, Lily, Deloris,
Jan, Hazel Anne, and Cathryn*

The Leadership Institute
http://www.theleadershipinstitute.org